Unmasking the
Watchtower
Who are the
Jehovah's Witnesses?

Selwyn R. Stevens, Ph.D.

D1640319

PUBLISHED BY

© Selwyn R. Stevens, 1994, 1996, 2000, 2007, 2015, 2018

Additional copies of this book are available from many bookstores, or from:

Jubilee Resources International Inc.
PO Box 3, Feilding 4740, New Zealand

or our secure Internet Webshop at
www.jubileeresources.org

ISBN 978-1877463-02-0

Unless otherwise indicated, all Scriptures are taken from The Holy Bible, New King James Version. Copyright 1990, 1985, 1983, by Thomas Nelson, Inc.

Scriptures in boxes on pages 28, 32, & 34 are from the 1985 edition of the Kingdom Inter-linear Translation of the Greek Scriptures, otherwise known as the New World Translation, used exclusively by the Watchtower Bible & Tract Society.

The author uses American English spelling, not the Queen's English.

Your guarantee of accurate Information various sources and authorities have been quoted in good faith throughout this book.
Every attempt has been made to ensure these quotations are accurate and in context.

CONTENTS

Foreword

"Dr. Selwyn Stevens' investigative reporting on Jehovah's Witnesses offer hope to those confused by or trapped in these cultic beliefs and practices. This is the best book I have read on the subject."

M. Lynn Reddick, B.A.; M.Div.; M.Th.; Th.D.; Ph.D.
President, Covenant Bible Institute
President, Open Church Ministries
Georgia, USA

About Jubilee Resources International

God's commission for Jubilee Resources International is based on Ezekiel 33:1-9, and Luke 4:18-21. According to the Bible, Jubilee years were times of restitution. Debts were cancelled, slaves set free, families reunited and lost or forfeited inheritances restored. Every year was prophetic of the ministry of Jesus Christ. The Jubilee was proclaimed on the basis of the work of the High Priest on the Day of Atonement - so Jesus Christ's liberating ministry is founded on His atoning work. Jesus began His public ministry by reading the passage from the prophet Isaiah (Luke 4:18-21). All the liberties of the Jubilee year are now available to us through the redemptive work of Jesus Christ at Calvary, and we all have the responsibility to preach this Gospel of Redemption and Restoration to full Relationship with Yahweh/Father God. When Yeshua/Jesus Christ returns, God's people will be totally free from all sin, sickness and disease, death and curse. The Biblical Jubilee will then be fully realized.

Resources in print book, eBook, audio & video formats are available in English, with paper & eBooks in Spanish, German, French, Italian, Portuguese-Brazil, Polish, Russian, Dutch, Swedish, Danish, Finnish, Hungarian, Romanian, Slovak, Czech, Greek, Afrikaans & Tagalog, with other languages pending.

INTRODUCTION

My priority in this series of book, "Unmasking Deception," is three-fold: First, it is intended to inform and equip Christians about groups that claim to be Christian, but which can be clearly shown are not. Such groups are often called cults. The short definition of a cult is *"A group of people who are gathered around someone's misinterpretation of the Bible,"* according to Dr. Walter Martin, probably the world's top Christian expert on cults. My hope is that many more Christians will learn to share their faith in Jesus Christ with effective Bible teaching and testimony, for the sake of the Kingdom of God. I also hope the Christian Church will see cults not as a threat but potentially as an essential mission field.

Secondly, I hope to provide compelling information which would cause a person considering joining the Watchtower organization to see that they are in danger of deception, and in all probability will jeopardise their eternal salvation, which is available only through faith in Jesus Christ, as revealed in the Bible. **"Beware lest anyone cheat you through philosophy and empty deceit, according to the tradition of men, according to the basic principles of this world, and not according to Christ. For in Him (Jesus) dwells all the fullness of the Godhead bodily; and you are complete in Him, who is the head of all principality and power,"** (Colossians 2:8-10).

Thirdly, it is my fervent prayer that those entangled in cults and other spiritual deceptions will recognize there is a salvation-threatening difference between what they are being taught in their group, and what God teaches us through His trustworthy word, the Bible. The challenge to each of us comes from the Bible. **"Examine yourselves as to whether you are in the faith. Prove yourselves. Do you not know yourselves, that Jesus Christ is in you? - unless indeed you are disqualified,"** (2 Corinthians 13:5). We are endangered when a man-made organization, such as the Watchtower, replaces Jesus Christ as the object of our worship and the reason for our activity. God instructs us in the Bible to test all things to see if they be of God. How can a Jehovah's Witness know they are testing all things if you are not permitted to read anything critical or even investigative of the Watchtower?

The point needs to be made that deceived people don't usually know they are. That is the nature of deception. Christians have a job to do with all speed; to know their God and His Word much better, so they can share with others the hope and love that they have in Jesus Christ. My prayer is that this series may assist in some small way to achieve that purpose.

Selwyn Stevens
New Zealand

WHO ARE THE JEHOVAH'S WITNESSES?

They were arguably the world's most active cult for several decades. They have congregations in 233 countries or territories. They are often referred to as the Watchtower Society, so both terms may be used interchangeably.

The Watchtower Society had been growing at a phenomenal rate around much of the world. Members of the Watchtower organization are taught they must "witness" for the group by going door-to-door sharing their version of religious belief. Their local bases are called Kingdom Halls.

In 1975 the Witnesses placed over 334 million pieces of literature in people's homes.

They are now losing adherents (primarily through disillusionment with their false prophecies and an increasing realization that Jesus Christ is Jehovah God,) their growth worldwide stalled during the 2010's and has begun to reduce steadily. Their 2020 membership of 8.4 million is down from their high of 11+million only a decade earlier.

In both New Zealand and Australia, every congregation of Jehovah's Witnesses averaged around 1,200 hours of door-to-door evangelism every month over the past few years. Worldwide this figure is a little less. Despite this, they lost ground or had no increase in 35 countries and territories, including Britain, Austria, Denmark, Fiji, France, Germany, Netherlands and Sweden. In New Zealand, expulsions exceeded new members during the last several years, mainly for asking the questions

I have posed in this book, at least that is what I am told. In fact several Kingdom Halls have recently closed, and at least one became a mosque. The erosion of membership in New Zealand has forced them to sell their large headquarters, and reestablish that in Australia.

Their growth rate was greatest in the former Communist countries of eastern Europe. Significant strength and growth are in countries where a majority of the population are Roman Catholic, particularly in Europe, Africa and Central and South America.

The Watchtower Society was outlawed in New Zealand in 1940, and in Australia in 1941, being described then as a "subversive organization." In January 1947 the Supreme Court of Canada ruled they "were not a religious body," and the same year the Watchtower was banned in Southern Rhodesia (now Zimbabwe).[2] The Watchtower Society was later allowed back to those countries. Newspaper reports indicate they have since been banned in Singapore. They have now been banned in Russia, China, Laos, Vietnam and almost all Moslem nations (see map).

The Jehovah's Witnesses weren't always known as that. Originally they were called Millennial Dawn, then they became Metropolitan Pulpit, then Brooklyn Tabernacle Pulpit, followed by the International Bible Students Association, then Zion Watchtower Society, then Watchtower Bible & Tract Society, until finally in 1931 their present name was given by a spirit guide.[1]

THE FOUNDING FATHER

The founder of the Watchtower Society, Charles Taze Russell, organized a Bible class in Pittsburgh when he was only 18. Although he never received any theological training the group later elected Russell as their pastor. Russell inherited a number of men's clothing stores in his earlier days and was quite good at business.

At a young age Russell became obsessed with the subject of hell. When an atheist friend apparently confused him too much Russell became an agnostic, but was later

Founder Charles T. Russell

brought back to some measure of faith by a member of the Seventh-Day Adventist church. He was particularly influenced by their teaching on Christ's second coming and the events prior to Armageddon. It seems Russell borrowed many of his beliefs from the Seventh-Day Adventists and the Christadelphians of his day, including that Jesus Christ was just Michael the Archangel, a created being. Russell later broke away from the Seventh-Day Adventists. Russell began publishing what is now known as the Watchtower magazine in 1879.

Russell wrote and spoke widely, and denounced all Christian churches, claiming they were being run by the devil. Russell sued an Ontario Baptist pastor, J.J. Ross, in 1912 after Ross published a pamphlet exposing Russell. Russell had falsely claimed he was an ordained minister who knew Greek. Under oath he failed to identify Greek letters put to him, and also had to admit to perjury and not knowing Hebrew or Latin either.[3]

In the following year Russell made a serious mistake by advertising what he called "Miracle Wheat" for sale at four times the normal price. The Brooklyn Daily Eagle newspaper exposed this fraud and was taken

Russell's pyramid tombstone, with the Knight's Templar Masonic insignia

to court by Russell for libel. When tested by the Government, the wheat was shown to be miraculous all right - miraculously low in quality. The newspaper won.

One of the more interesting facts to come out of this case was that the Watchtower organization was nothing more than a moneymaking scheme for Russell.[4] All the subsidiary societies passed their profits along to a holding company which had three shareholders, Russell who owned 99% of the shares and two other people owned one percent between them. I wonder who gets all that money now? That same year Russell's wife, Maria, sued him for divorce on grounds of "...*his conceit, egotism, domination and improper conduct towards other women.*"[5]

My purpose in mentioning Russell's dishonesty is not to be vindictive, but to check out the credibility of a man who claimed to have the only correct interpretation of God's Word. Human beings let us down, but it is God alone who is worthy of our full trust. Russell became more and more extreme as he grew older, predicting that all schools, churches, banks and the American Government would be destroyed by October 1914. When that didn't happen the date was moved to 1925. Russell would be dead nine years before the second date was also proven false. Russell was deported from Canada in 1916 for attempting to hinder their military mobilization required for World War One.

PRESIDENTS OF THE WATCHTOWER

Joseph Rutherford

Joseph Rutherford became president in 1917. He was referred to as "Judge" Rutherford, but this claim is rather tenuous as he served only briefly as a special judge in Missouri. Although he only reached the seventh grade at school, Rutherford did practice law. The domineering Rutherford was fierce in his unrelenting attacks on Christianity. The previously democratic Society was strongly centralized to convert the Brooklyn headquarters into a type of Watchtower Vatican, with significant control over their membership.

A number of the more extreme doctrines arose during Rutherford's time. Along with seven other leading Witnesses, Rutherford was convicted and imprisoned for several months towards the end of 1918 for inciting Witnesses to avoid being drafted into the American armed forces. Witnesses got around this in World War Two by claiming all members have the title "Minister," a practice continued to this day.[6]

After Rutherford died in 1942 Nathan Knorr became the third leader. During Knorr's 35 years as president his style of behind-the-scenes organizer and equipper of his people saw growth from 100,000 to over 2.25 million. Under Knorr's leadership vast quantities of printed literature began to be distributed and sold around the world, a practice still continuing.

Nathan Knorr

Frederick Franz became the Watchtower president

Frederick Franz

in 1977, and his death in 1993 saw support exceed 11 million. It is remarkable there have been only four leaders in 120 years. Franz probably faced more crises than the others as many Witnesses searched their Bibles and history to understand the many false prophecies which were starting to be obvious, even to many Witnesses. The first decade of Franz's presidency saw over 1 million witnesses leave or be expelled (disfellowshipped).

Milton Henschel

Milton Henschel was then selected as the president, despite being in his eighties. The Watchtower have a Governing Body of 15 men (no equal opportunity here) who are very authoritarian, and go to great lengths to retain the image of divine guidance. Strict obedience to the Governing Body's decisions is essential if members wish to continue attending local Kingdom Halls. Questioning of the Governing Body and other Watchtower authorities, no matter how honestly, is not permitted.

When Henschel stepped down in 2000, Don Adams succeeded him as president until he died in 2014, and was succeeded by Robert Ciranko,, who died of Covid in 2020. No successor has been named at time of print, but the management of a board of eight members has been put into place.

The Watchtower & Awake magazines are the main tools Jehovah's Witnesses use for teaching error. The left copy shows the Knights' Templar cross & crown in the top left corner, insignia for a well-known Masonic order

GOD'S CHANNEL?

Most Watchtower publications make the bold claim to be God's sole channel for communication on earth - Jehovah's prophet.[7]

The Prophecies of the Watchtower

6,000 years of human history would end in:
1872, 1873, 1972, 1975

The Millennium will begin in:
1873, 1874, now very soon

Armageddon due:
1914, 1915, 1918, 1925, 1941, 1975, now very soon

The First Resurrection will be in:
1878, 1925, 1926, 1972, 1975

In the 3 years from May 1940 they made at least 44 predictions about the imminence of Armageddon. Christ's (invisible) return was claimed to be in 1874, and this date was taught by the Watchtower until at least 1927.9 This particular date was connected to the Millerite movement which birthed the Seventh Day Adventists. When membership started falling because of the false dates given for so many "prophecies," Christ's return was amended to 1914. When that didn't happen either they said he had in fact returned but invisibly to Brooklyn, New York, which happens to be their headquarters. This is contradicted by the Bible which says, **"He is coming in the clouds, and every eye will see**

Classic example of a false prophecy

An interesting issue of the Watchtower magazine that was sent to me by one of their members. Will they take their own advice? How will they know if they aren't permitted to read anything that investigates the Watchtower Society?

Him, and they also who pierced Him..." (Revelation 1:7). There is nothing invisible there.

The Biblical standard for judging false prophets is plain: **"But the prophet who presumes to speak a word in My name, which I have not commanded him to speak, or who speaks in the name of other gods, that prophet shall die. And if you say in your heart, 'How shall we know the word which the LORD has not spoken?' When a prophet speaks in the name of the LORD, if the thing does not happen or come to pass, that is the thing which the LORD has not spoken; the prophet has spoken it presumptuously; you shall not be afraid of him." (Deuteronomy 18:20-22).**

God's instruction in Deuteronomy 13:1-8. is that anyone who pretends to speak for Him and whose prophecies fail to happen are to be put to death. According to Jeremiah 23:40, false prophets face everlasting shame and being cast out of God's presence. 2 Peter 1:20-21 also provides instructions about prophecies.

"If the message Jehovah's Witnesses are bringing to the people is true, then it is of the greatest importance to mankind. If it is false then it is the duty of the clergymen and others who support them to come boldly forward and plainly tell the people wherein the message is false,"[8]

This is a rare challenge for investigation from Joseph Rutherford. That is one of the main purposes of this book. The Watchtower of February 1, 1992 also warned readers to avoid false prophets. This raises some interesting questions, because if the Watchtower is a False Prophet, then Jehovah's Witnesses are commanded not to read their own literature. Here are a few of the better documented of the Watchtower's false or "evolving prophecies."

In their 1975 yearbook it stated that for over a century *"...Jehovah's servants have enjoyed spiritual enlightenment and direction."* The Watchtower claims that the light of their understanding is getting brighter and brighter, so when they get something wrong, a later enlightenment will improve their understanding. That is saying that truth gets more true. But truth is unchangeable, not flexible like the Watchtower's teaching and prophecies. There is a serious credibility problem here; either Jehovah God keeps changing His mind a great deal, or the leaders of the Watchtower are bringing false prophecies. The real truth is that the Watchtower Society of Jehovah's Witnesses have proclaimed more false prophecies than any other religious cult I have researched. In fact, I have yet to confirm a single event they have prophesied which has actually happened. The evidence is very clear that those who speak for the Watchtower Society have the marks of a false prophet, measured by the standard God clearly laid down in the Bible.

Not everyone desires to hear from them, as these two posters indicate.

CHRISTIAN BELIEFS?

For many years the followers of the Watchtower have claimed to be Christians, although there is an increasing rejection of that title over recent times. Let us compare some of the major Bible doctrines to see how the Watchtower measures up.

THE WATCHTOWER   CHRISTIANITY

What is the Holy Bible?

They claim the Bible has many mistakes.& They also claim their "New World Translation" is better.

It is the trustworthy Word of God the final authority for doctrine and truth. (2 Tim. 3:16; 2 Peter 1:20-21; Proverbs 30:5; Romans 16:25-26)

Who is the Godhead?

There is only one God - Jehovah. God is singular, there is no Trinity.

There is one God who chooses to reveal Himself as 3 persons, The Father, The Son and The Holy Spirit (Genesis 1:26; Matthew 28:19; 3:16-17; Luke 1:35)

Who is Jesus Christ?

Not God, but Michael the archangel, He was "a god." The first being God ever created.

Jesus is God the Son, 2nd person of the Trinity. While on earth He remained 100% God yet also 100% man. He is sinless and uniquely able to save people. (John 1:1,14; 1 Timothy 3:16)

Who is the Holy Spirit?

The Holy Spirit is not a person or God but an "it" - just the 'power of God.' an invisible active force, likened beam.

God the Holy Spirit is the 3rd person in the trinity, the Comforter and the provider of spiritual gifts. to a radar (Acts 5:1-4; Hebrews 3:7-11; 1 Corinthians 12:3-11)

THE WATCHTOWER	CHRISTIANITY

What effect does the Blood of Jesus have?

Christ's life was a perfect human life; No more or less. He was not God	Because Jesus was sinless, His blood was shed for the forgiveness (atonement) of everyone who believes in Him. (1 John 1:7; Revelation 1:5;Romans 3:23;5:9)

What is Salvation?

Comes through good works and by being a Jehovah's Witness. Grace is devalued.	Salvation cannot be earned by what we do, but by our indivicual acceptance of the atoning work of Jesus Christ through His death, burial & resurrection. (Eph, 2:8-9; Galatians 2:16; Titus 3:5)

What about the Resurrection of Jesus Christ?

There was no bodily resurrection of Jesus, and man will not be resurrected either. The sinful will be annihilated.	Jesus was physically resurrected with a glorified body, and this is God's f promise or all believers in Christ at His return. (Luke 24:36,39; John 2:19,21; 1 Corinthians 15:3-8,42,44)

Is Jesus Christ Returning?

The invisible presence of Christ returned to earth in 1914, and will be visible at Armageddon to rule for 1,000 years.	At a time undisclosed but promised in the Bible, Jesus will physically and visibly return to earth to establish His kingdom. (Rev. 1:7; Matthew 24:30; 1 Thess. 4:15-17; Acts 1:9-11)

What is Salvation?

Only 144,000 Jehovah's Witnesses will go to heaven. An eternal hell of conscious torment does not exist. Righteous J. W.'s will live on earth with Christ, and all others will be annihilated.	There are only two eternal destinations for mankind: in heaven with God, or in hell in conscious torment. The choice is ours. (Hebrews 9:27; Matthew 25:34,41; Revelation 14:9-11, 20:10-15)

The Virgin Birth

Jesus was conceived by an invisible active force (called The Holy Spirit) who is not a person and is not God.	Jesus was conceived by God the Holy Spirit in the Virgin Mary's womb. (Matt.1:18-20, Luke 1:35, Isaiah 7:14).

DOCTRINES THAT CHANGE

The presidents of the Jehovah's Witnesses have claimed power to speak for God at a level equal to or greater than the Roman Catholic Pope when he speaks Ex Cathedra or infallibly. Every president has changed the doctrines to suit himself. Let us look at a few of these.

Teaching	Was	Now
Blood Transfusions	okay	forbidden
Vaccinations	forbidden	okay
"Faithful & Wise Servant"	Russell	Watchtower
Book of Ruth	history	prophecy
Abaddon	Jesus	Satan
Worship of Jesus	encouraged	discouraged
Resurrection	for all	144,000 only
Israel	physical nation	believers only
"Superior Authorities"	political rulers	Jehovah

(the Superior Authorities are now back to being the political rulers again.)[10]

One scholar recorded 148 changes of official Watchtower doctrine during the 11 years following 1917. At least one Scripture (Luke 16:19-31) has so far been interpreted five different ways, with one interpretation only lasting two months.[11]

DOES THE BIBLE LEAD TO DARKNESS?

Charles Russell wrote in the Watchtower magazine in 1910 that if you read the Bible on its own it will lead you into darkness. One Witness explained to me that this statement was a mistake which they have since put right. If that is so, why did the Watchtower magazine of August 15, 1981 say the same thing? It plainly stated that reading the Bible without reading the Watchtower literature would result in you believing what the Christian Church has been teaching for 2,000 years.

What the Watchtower is claiming is that Jehovah God can't write and explain His word clearly. Is God so powerless that He cannot grant us understanding through His Holy Spirit? There may be parts we don't yet fully understand, but God invites us to ask the Holy Spirit to help us with the meaning and implications of His Word. The evidence is that the Watchtower is giving a private, exclusive and frequently erroneous interpretation of the Bible. It is God who should give us understanding of the Bible, not the Watchtower (1 John 2:27). Sometimes God will use a human teacher such as Philip when he taught the Eunuch from Ethiopia in Acts 8:26-38. When Philip taught the true gospel of who Jesus is, the man was saved and baptized. God is not limited in how He teaches us, unless we seek to limit Him ourselves.

Since the profits of the 380 million Watchtower and Awake magazines, plus all the books sold, provide about 67% of the annual income of the Watchtower Society,[26] I am left wondering what their real motive is. That adds up to a lot of spare money. I have yet to locate any evidence of their accounting for all this money. The cynic might ask if this money is required to keep the leaders in a high and inappropriate lifestyle, such as Joseph Rutherford's palatial mansion "Beth Sarim" in California - however that is another story the Watchtower's Governing Body wish to hide from their members.

THE NAME OF GOD

Joseph Rutherford was the first to teach that God's only true and correct name is "Jehovah." The only problem is that the name Jehovah doesn't occur in the original Hebrew or Greek Bible, because the word for "God" is "ADONAI" which translates to "LORD." The Hebrews would never speak His name, for it was claimed to be too holy to be uttered. When they wrote it down

they used "YHWH." (Hebrew language has no vowels.) Nowadays this name is written as "YAHWEH," (pronounced Yarway). When Moses asked God who He was, God answered, **"I AM who I AM... This is My name forever,"** (Exodus 3:14-15). Since then, further names of God have been used which reflect His character.

In 1270 AD, a Catholic monk named Raymundus Martini decided to add the vowels from Adonai to the Latinized YHWH (JHVH), and so invented the name "JEHOVAH."[14] Although this name has been moderately popular ever since, the fact remains that it still isn't in the Bible, (apart from some editions of the King James Bible where it was inserted in place of Adonai), nor is it the name God gave of Himself. Jehovah is not the exclusive name of God, as Rutherford falsely claimed, and many Watchtower leadership and members are still claiming.

WHO MUST WE PRAY TO?
People in cults (including Jehovah's Witnesses) need to understand one very important fact. No-one can reach God unless they go through Jesus Christ! When a Witness prays they are taught that only the elect 144,000 have Jesus as a mediator.[17] No

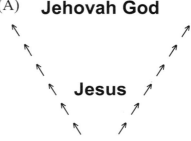

(A) **Jehovah God**

Jesus

Jehovah's Witness

one else has any mediator. So that means God cannot answer all the others' prayers. Let me show you what I mean. When a Witness prays this is what happens. (A)

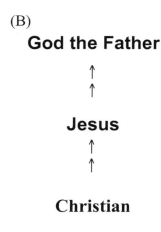

(B)

God the Father

↑
↑

Jesus

↑
↑

Christian

The Witness may say, *"We cannot pray to Jesus. Where does it say we can pray to Jesus?"* Acts 7:59, 1 Corinthians 1:2 are just two examples of where we can pray to Christ. But when a Christian prays, (B) 1 Timothy 2:5 says that Jesus is our mediator, so He takes our prayers and gives them to the Father. Jesus only does this for people who have put their faith in Him. God the Father says we must have that relationship with Jesus, because without it, we can't reach the Father.

"Jehovah's Witnesses of today are in the same position of unbelief as the rejecting Jews of the New Testament. They deny the deity and bodily resurrection of Christ, and they oppose the church of Christ. In so doing, they reject the work of the Holy Spirit within every believer," according to author Philip Elliot[28]

144,000, DEATH, HELL AND THE FUTURE

A famous writer once wrote, *"The statistics are very impressive - one out of every one dies."* The Watchtower claim there are three groups of people. First there is an exclusive or heavenly congregation, usually called "The Anointed Class" or "The Little Flock." This class is limited to 144,000 people and was filled up by 1935, according to Joseph Rutherford.[15] That means there are fewer than 5,000 still alive. More recent information suggests the Watchtower leadership have begun to increase the number admitted to this exclusive list. No explanation has yet been made as to the method used for adding to this list. These select people are required to undergo sacrifice and suffering modelled after Jesus Christ, so their salvation comes after their baptism and obedience to Watchtower rules, and proving themselves worthy. Jesus is their mediator. Following Armageddon these people are taken to heaven, or so it is claimed.

The second group are the other good Watchtower members and people of goodwill, who are called "Jonadabs."[16] After Armageddon it is claimed these people will be placed on a restored earth. The third group, all the rest of us humans, are supposed to experience annihilation - a cessation of existence. These last two groups have no mediator with God.

The Bible does not teach any of the above. The Bible reveals that the 144,000 mentioned in Revelation 7:4-8, consist of twelve thousand from each of the twelve tribes of Israel - so they are Jewish, not the elite Watchtower leaders. Revelation 14:4 states emphatically these 144,000 are **"virgins not defiled by women,"** which means they are unmarried, celibate and male. Many Watchtower members in the 144,000 are married, and some are women. The Watchtower leaders have deceived themselves, and their members, again.

It is helpful to remember there is no limit recorded in the Bible as to the number of people who can be saved. **"Whoever believes that Jesus is the Christ (Messiah) is born of God..."** (1 John 5:1). "Unless one is born of water and the Spirit, he cannot enter the kingdom of God," (John 3:5). So Jesus is telling us God's Kingdom is open to whoever believes. The Faith Hall of Fame of Hebrews 11 shows these men and women of God were looking for a heavenly destination, not an earthly one.

Nowhere in the Bible is physical death portrayed as the extinction of a human being. Jesus tells us about the rich man and Lazarus being conscious of their state after death in Luke 16:23. Jesus also stated that it would have been better if Judas had never been born in Matthew 26:24. Jesus' comments would only have meaning if there is existence after death. The Bible teaches that the soul continues to exist after physical death (Matthew 17:3, Revelation 6:9-11, & 1 Samuel 28:18-19). Jesus warns us not to fear those who can kill the body but who have no power over the soul (Matthew 10:28).

Part of the problem Jehovah's Witnesses have is their rejection of Holy Spirit. Jesus stated that Holy Spirit is our teacher and revelator. We can't understand the Bible without Him and that is why Jehovah's Witnesses don't understand, meaning their "inspiration" must be from demons.

There are two deaths - a physical one, and a spiritual one. Physical death sees the body buried or cremated. The person's soul and spirit then go to one of two places. If that person chose Jesus as Lord and Savior while alive, these return to God who gave them in the first place. If, however, that person failed to choose Jesus, their soul and spirit reside in Hades, the place of the unsaved dead, to await the Great White Throne Judgement of Revelation 20. That is the final judgement of the damned, prior to their entry into the Lake of Fire.

Human beings are a spirit and have a soul, and it is by our spirit that we become children of God, because a Born-Again spirit never dies, (John 3:5-6, Galatians 6:8, & 1 Corinthians 5:5). From Genesis onwards, there is no such promise of eternal life for those unsaved.

If physical death means annihilation, as the Watchtower and Christadelphians both teach, then Jesus was made extinct at Calvary. He could not rise from the dead, and can never return to this earth, in 1874, 1914 or any other time. God would have had to replace Jesus, not rebuild Him as Michael. Annihilation is total destruction, not some sort of limbo prior to reconstruction. Any dictionary will confirm that.

It is interesting that almost all cults reject the idea of hell. The Mormons believe in a spirit prison remarkably similar to the false Roman Catholic doctrine of Purgatory. These beliefs claim a person's spirit can be released to go to a better spiritual abode after death, usually paradise or a higher level of heaven. The Watchtower also teach something similar, as they claim that Witnesses will "educate" billions of people during the Millennium so they can choose to accept or reject Jehovah on Judgement Day. But 1 Corinthians 15 shows that only believers in Jesus Christ will be resurrected on His return. Revelation 20 shows that after the 1,000 year reign of Jesus on this earth (called the Millennium) everyone will be resurrected for judgement, and **"Anyone not found written in the Book of Life was cast into the lake of fire,"** (Revelation 20:15). That's also where those who reject salvation in Jesus Christ. Scripture shows this entails eternal separation from God. These will be consumed by the fire until they are no more. Annihilation can't occur prior to then. That's why Scripture calls it **"The Second Death."** (Revelation. 21:8).

The Bible is clear - there can be no change in our spiritual state after our physical death. That is why it is important to choose Jesus now.

Hell is a hot place of eternal torment, and it is real. God designed Hell as a place of eternal punishment for those angels who rebelled against Him and supported Lucifer. I have found no Biblical evidence which even hints that God intended human beings to go there. Please make sure you don't join them!

607 BC AND ALL THAT

In a vain attempt to justify their claim that Jesus returned to earth in 1914, the Watchtower teach that Jerusalem was destroyed by Nebuchadnezzer in 607BC. This is claimed to be 2520 years by a complicated method of calculation (from Daniel chapter 4), for which I don't have the space here to explain. The problem is that Nebuchadnezzer didn't become king until early September of 605BC, two years after he was supposed to have invaded and destroyed Jerusalem. *"The siege of Jerusalem ended in its capture in August 586BC."*[12] This was followed by two deportations of prominent citizens.

I have yet to locate a reliable history book with any date which varies more than twelve months from 586BC. Former Watchtower Governing Body member, Raymond Franz (nephew of President Frederick Franz) admits there is no historical evidence to support the 607BC date. He wrote that this date was only maintained by the Watchtower because it would be too embarrassing to admit they couldn't count.[13]

BIG QUESTIONS

This raises serious questions for every Jehovah Witness. How do you know that what you are told to be true today won't be declared false tomorrow? Or what you are told is false today won't be declared true tomorrow? The Bible is very clear that God cannot lie (1 Samuel 15;29 & Romans 3:4) and that He is unchanging and unchangeable (Malachi 3:6 & James 1:17). God is not the author of confusion (1 Corinthians 14:33). It is clear that the "spiritual enlightenment" claimed by the Leaders of the Watchtower organization cannot have come from God. The source of their confusion is either soulish, or inspired by Satan himself. It does show that anyone who chooses to get involved with the Watchtower does so at the risk of deception.

SCHOLARS' CREDENTIALS

Publications by the Watchtower Society neglect to list the names and credentials of their authors or major contributors, even their *"New World Translation."* The excuse given is that they don't seek the approval of men, but of Jehovah God. This makes it almost impossible to establish the credentials of their contributors. However, every recognized Bible translation and Christian book contains details of translators and/or authors, and their credentials. This way phony experts can be challenged and exposed, while true authorities may have their work verified.

Watchtower President F.W. Franz, along with (former) president Nathan Knorr, headed the secret committee of seven translators. Franz testified in a court case in Edinburgh, Scotland, November 23, 1954. The "Scottish Daily Express" on November 24, 1954, recorded his testimony word for word. In Franz's testimony he stated under oath:

1. That he and Knorr had the final word in translation;
2. That he (Franz) was head of the Society's publicity department;
3. That translations and interpretations came from God, invisibly communicated to the publicity department by *"angels of various ranks who control[led]"* the translators.[29]

This is a rather startling admission. What Franz is describing is not divine inspiration but spiritism. These angels must be unholy or demonic, because only they would have so twisted the translation of the Bible in that way. One Spiritist "translator" of the Bible, who freely claimed that his translation originated in the "spirit world," was Johannes Greber, a former German Catholic priest. His 1937 New Testament is the source of many New World Translation passages, including John 1:1 and Hebrews 1:8, etc. This proves that the Watchtower, while officially claiming opposition to spiritism, are actually using it in their translation work. That is the most likely reason why Watchtower publications like the New World Translation decline to list the contributors. No wonder they want to hide that from their members.

THE NEW WORLD TRANSLATION

It would be helpful to look at Watchtower's New World Translation of the Bible. What do the experts, Christian and non-Christian, think of the NWT?

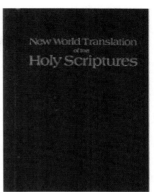

* *"I have never read any New Testament so badly translated as the (NWT) Kingdom Interlinear Translation of the Greek Scriptures,"* (Dr. Julius Mantey).18

* *"It is abundantly clear that a sect which can translate the New Testament like that is intellectually dishonest,"* (Dr. William Barclay).[19]

* *"From beginning to end this volume (NWT) is a shining example of how the Bible should not be translated..."* (Dr.H.H. Rowley).[20]

* *"It must be stated quite frankly that, if the Jehovah's Witnesses take this translation seriously, they are polytheists,"* (Professor Bruce Metzger).[21]

* The Watchtower *"Has been sharply unsuccessful in keeping doctrinal considerations from influencing the actual translation... it must be viewed as a radically biased piece of work. At some points it is actually dishonest. At others it is neither modern nor scholarly,"* (Dr. Robert Countess).[22]

Despite the Bible's firm declaration that Jesus and the Holy Spirit are both part of the Triune God, the Watchtower reject these Bible doctrines and have issued a translation into which they have forced a bias to fit their beliefs. In all my research I have yet to find one genuine Hebrew or Greek scholar or translator of the Bible who supports the Watchtower version. The only authorities the Witnesses have been able to quote are Unitarian or Spiritualists and since both are anti-Christian their claims have no credibility.

Space permits only one example of this blatant altering of the Bible

COLOSSIANS 1:16—21   880

εἰκὼν   τοῦ   θεοῦ   τοῦ   ἀοράτου,   πρωτότοκος
image   of the   God   the   invisible,   firstborn

πάσης   κτίσεως,   16   ὅτι   ἐν   αὐτῷ
of all   creation,   because   in   him

ἐκτίσθη   τὰ   πάντα   ἐν τοῖς οὐρανοῖς
it was created   the   all (things)   in   the   heavens.

καὶ   ἐπὶ   τῆς   γῆς,   τὰ   ὁρατὰ   καὶ
and   upon   the   earth,   the (things)   visible   and

τὰ   ἀόρατα,   εἴτε   θρόνοι   εἴτε
the (things)   invisible,   whether   thrones   or

κυριότητες   εἴτε   ἀρχαὶ   εἴτε   ἐξουσίαι·
lordships   or   governments   or   authorities;

τὰ   πάντα   δι'   αὐτοῦ καὶ   εἰς   αὐτὸν
the   all (things)   through   him   and   into   him

ἔκτισται·   17   καὶ   αὐτός   ἐστιν   πρὸ
it has been created;   and   he   is   before

πάντων   καὶ   τὰ   πάντα   ἐν   αὐτῷ
all (things)   and   the   all (things)   in   him

συνέστηκεν,   18   καὶ   αὐτός   ἐστιν   ἡ
it has stood together,   and   he   is   the

κεφαλὴ   τοῦ   σώματος,   τῆς   ἐκκλησίας·
head   of the   body,   of the   ecclesia;

ὅς   ἐστιν   ἡ   ἀρχή,   πρωτότοκος   ἐκ
who   is   the   beginning,   firstborn   out of

τῶν   νεκρῶν,   ἵνα   γένηται   ἐν
the   dead (ones),   in order that   might become   in

πᾶσιν   αὐτὸς   πρωτεύων,
all (things)   he   holding the first place,

19   ὅτι   ἐν   αὐτῷ   εὐδόκησεν   πᾶν   τὸ
because   in   him   he thought well   all   the

πλήρωμα   κατοικῆσαι   20   καὶ   δι'   αὐτοῦ
fullness   to dwell down   and   through   him

ἀποκαταλλάξαι   τὰ   πάντα   εἰς   αὐτόν,
to reconcile   the   all (things)   into   him,

εἰρηνοποιήσας   διὰ   τοῦ   αἵματος   τοῦ
having made peace   through   the   blood   of the

σταυροῦ   αὐτοῦ,   δι'   αὐτοῦ   εἴτε
stake   of him,   through   him   whether

τὰ   ἐπὶ   τῆς   γῆς   εἴτε   τὰ   ἐν
the (things)   upon   the   earth   or   the (things)   in

τοῖς   οὐρανοῖς.
the   heavens.

the image of the invisible God, the firstborn of all creation; 16 because by means of him all [other] things were created in the heavens and upon the earth, the things visible and the things invisible, no matter whether they are thrones or lordships or governments or authorities. All [other] things have been created through him and for him. 17 Also, he is before all [other] things and by means of him all [other] things were made to exist, 18 and he is the head of the body, the congregation. He is the beginning, the firstborn from the dead, that he might become the one who is first in all things; 19 because [God] saw good for all fullness to dwell in him, 20 and through him to reconcile again to himself all [other] things by making peace through the blood [he shed] on the torture stake,* no matter whether they are the things upon the earth or the

New World Translation of the Kingdom Interlinear Bible, used exclusively by Watchtower adherents. See underlined insertion of false word

text to show what I mean. Colossians 1:15 onwards speaks of Jesus as **"the image of the invisible God,"** and goes on to state that Jesus created ALL things. In several of these verses (please see passage above) the Watchtower have inserted the word [other] to imply that Jesus was first created prior to creating everything else. But the Bible doesn't say that, and neither does the Greek/English version right beside it on the same page. The word [other] is inserted deliberately to make it say something different than what it really does say. This shows blatant dishonesty by the Watchtower leaders.

THE JESUS OF THE WATCHTOWER

So what do the Jehovah's Witnesses believe concerning Jesus Christ? They believe He was the first creation of Jehovah God, and He was the archangel Michael who was later changed into the mortal man Jesus. After His death they claim Jesus was changed back into Michael. Witnesses are taught *"Jesus received immortality as a reward for his faithful course of action [on earth]."*[23] The Witnesses also claim that Jesus was not resurrected physically but rather spiritually. They say Jesus cannot return physically to earth because his body disintegrated. Having got themselves into that corner they have to say that their Jesus/ Michael returned spiritually in 1914. I challenge any Jehovah's Witness to give me just one Bible verse which says Michael will return to earth!

If Jesus was only a man why is He called the "Lord of Glory" in 1 Corinthians 2:8? If Jesus was just a man, a created being, why did He forgive sins in Matthew 9:2, Mark 3:5, Luke 5:20, Luke 7:48 and elsewhere? If Jesus was not physically resurrected then the whole Christian faith is false and all the writers of the New Testament were telling lies too, according to 1 Corinthians chapter 15. Verse 15 of that chapter describes the teachers of the Watchtower as "false witnesses" on this very point.

Some claim the body of Jesus is still in a tomb. The Jews and the Romans would have produced it if it had been there to produce, if only to stop this talk about Jesus rising from the dead. Were the 500 people who claimed to see Jesus after His death all telling lies? Would the disciples be prepared to die for a lie, if they believed that Jesus was still dead? No way!

Matthew 24:1-35 and verses elsewhere state that Jesus will return physically to earth and the entire world will recognize Jesus. The Bible says that Jesus will appear visibly and physically - not invisibly and spiritually. The Bible says that Jesus will appear in the same body He had while on earth, although it is now glorified, (See John 20:24-28; Acts 1:9-11; Zechariah 12:10.) Those Scriptures are conclusive evidence that the Christ of the Jehovah's Witnesses cannot be the Christ of the Bible!

FIRST-BORN OR FIRST-CREATED

So how have the Witnesses got themselves into such a mess over the Bible? Have they never learned that you cannot use one part of the Biblical text to disprove or devalue another? God's Word is a whole message, it is equally inspired. As Dr. Derek Prince says *"a text out of context is a pretext,"* a lie! When we study a verse we need to study its context, maybe read the whole chapter or even the book. Proper contextual study like that would dissolve virtually every false teaching from cult groups such as the Watchtower Society.

Let's look at one example. We read before from Colossians chapter one verse 15 **"He [Jesus] is the image of the invisible God, the first-born over all creation."** When a Witness reads that they say that because this verse states that Jesus is the first-born, then he must have had a beginning even if it was right at the beginning of God's creative work. According to Dr. Bruce Metzger (Professor of New Testament Language and Literature, of Princeton, New Jersey) *"If Paul had wished to express the idea (that Christ was created) he had available a Greek word to do so, the word Protoktistos, meaning "first created." Actually, however, Paul uses the word prototokos, meaning "first begotten," which signifies something quite different."*[24]

Let us confirm this by looking at a Greek dictionary. Strong's shows that this word 'First-born' is "Prototokos," (Strong's 4416). This word means first in time, pre-eminence or privilege. A Scriptural example of this is in Psalm 89:27 where King David is described as the first-born of Jesse. But according to 1 Samuel 16:10 David was not the first-born but had seven brothers older than himself. David was first in pre-eminence as the anointed King. So Jesus is not the first-created being, but the first-born. First-born means pre-eminence in rank, not priority in time. A modern-day example would be the Prime Minister. He/she is not the first minister we have ever had, but they are currently the most important minister in the nation.

The answer to this issue of Jesus being described as the first-born is in verses 17 and 18; **"He is before all things"** and **"That in all things He may have pre-eminence."** Paul's use of the term "first-born" is intended to mean *"The Supreme One,"* the *"First in Authority."*

Jesus existed before all things were created. He created all things because he is God.

I think the Watchtower suffers from confusion between beget and create. To beget is to become the father of something like yourself. To create is to make something else. Consider the illustration by C.S. Lewis, *"A man begets human babies, a beaver begets little beavers, and a bird begets eggs which turn into little birds. But when you make, you make something of a different kind from yourself. A bird makes a nest, a beaver builds a dam, and a man makes... a statue."*[25] What God begets is God, and what man begets is child. That is why the Father calls His Son "GOD" in Hebrews 1:8. Jesus didn't cease to be God when He put on His humanity, but he functioned as a man so He could buy back what Adam had lost.

Please study the Scriptures I will now give you, check out their context, read the verses around them so you understand what God is saying. This will be an investment of time you won't regret. It is not too simple to state that the wrong understanding of who God really is the surest sign of a cult. The NWT version of some of these Scriptures is worded quite differently. In view of the Unitarian bias of the NWT, and its spiritist-inspired interpretation in places, it should not be considered suitable for serious Bible study.

WHO IS THE SAVIOR?

"I am the LORD your God... for there is no savior besides Me," (Hosea 13:4). Isaiah 43:11 states God is our only Savior. Verse 1 of the same chapter says it is God who creates and redeems us. Acts 4:12 tells us there is no other name than Jesus by which we must be saved! Colossians 1:16 and Ephesians 3:9 tell us that Jesus created us. The Bible is clear that Jesus fulfills the roles of Savior, Creator and Redeemer. That is why He is addressed as **"Our great God and Savior,"** in Titus 2:13. In Matthew 1:23 we are told that Jesus is **"Immanuel"** - God with us! Not a little part of God but fully God. The name 'Jesus,' or 'Yeshua' means 'God's Salvation.' Why not Michael's salvation? Because no created being can save us, no matter who falsely tells us otherwise.

"The LORD is our Judge, the LORD is our Lawgiver, the LORD

is our King; He will save us," (Isaiah 33:22). Let us consider the following:

* Jesus is our judge (John 5:22)
* Jesus completes and fulfils the Law (Matt. 5:17-18)
* Jesus is King of Kings and Lord of Lords (Rev. 19:16)
* Jesus is our Savior (Matthew 1:21)

Jesus possesses all the qualifications to be God. The Old Testament frequently translates God's name as "LORD." Yet in the New Testament, the only person who is consistently called "Lord" is Jesus Christ. Isn't that interesting!

THREE GODS OR ONE?

The Jehovah's Witnesses have written in several of their publications that Christians teach there are three gods. Actually the Mormons teach that, but Christians don't. What does the Bible actually say? Jehovah's Witnesses have been taught by their leaders that Jehovah is the only God, but that He created Jesus as a secondary and inferior God. That is polytheism. The Bible teaches there is only one God by nature, and all other "gods" are created and false (Galatians 4:8). **"This is eternal life, that they may know you, the only true God, and Jesus Christ whom you have sent,"** (John 17:3). (The context is Jesus praying to the Father and addressing Him as the One and Only True God.)

How many true Gods are there? Surely there is only one!

Would you agree that whatever is not true must be false? (YES.)

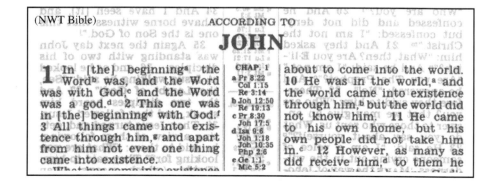

If there is only one true God then all other gods must be false gods, correct? (YES.)

I have yet to find a Bible scholar who claims that the "WORD" of John 1:1 is anyone other than Jesus Christ. Is Jesus a true god or a false god, because even in the New World Translation is plainly shows Jesus is "A GOD." If Jesus is a false god then both John and Thomas are guilty of falsely honoring Jesus as God, and this would be blasphemy if true. Not even Jehovah's Witnesses teach that. Therefore Jesus must be the true God. But Jehovah is the only true God. Simple logic demands that Jesus must be Jehovah! There can be no other deduction. It is impossible for a believer in the Bible to accept there are two true gods, but that is actually what the Watchtower teaches.

IN WHOSE NAME?

If you doubt what I have said then please tell me, from the Bible, the following;

* In whose name should believers meet? (Matt. 18:20, 1 Cor. 5:4).

* In whose name are demons subject? (Luke 10:17, Acts 16:18).

* In whose name is repentance and forgiveness to be preached? (Luke 24:47).

* In whose name are we to believe and receive forgiveness of sins? (John 1:12,3:16, Acts 10:43, 1 John 3:23, 5:13).

* In whose name and no other do we obtain salvation? (Acts 4:12).

* In whose name is the Holy Spirit sent? (John 14:26).

* In whose name and authority were the disciples to heal the sick? (Acts 3:16, 4:7-10,30).

* Whose name is above EVERY other name? (Eph. 1:21 Phil. 2:9-11).

* In whose name are we to witness? (Acts 1:8).

* In whose name are we to petition God in prayer? (John 14:13-14, 15:16, 16:23-24).

The Bible answer to every one of the above questions is JESUS of Nazareth!

I could have used a lot more Scriptures, maybe even better ones. I invite you to check these Scriptures out, and be convinced by God's word alone that Jesus is God. If you are genuine in seeking the truth about God then you need to understand there are three persons who are called God, and each of those persons has all the attributes of deity. Christians willingly accept the Scripture from Deuteronomy 6:4 which says: **"Sh'ma Yisra'el, Adonai Eloheinu, Adonai echad," "Here O Israel; the LORD our God, The LORD is One."** That is a wonderful truth. Have you ever wondered why God's name is mentioned three times in this verse? Maybe He is trying to tell us something, if we dare to listen to Him.

THE ALPHA AND THE OMEGA

Revelation 1:7-8 (box 1, all NWT) says that someone "is coming." Who? Verse 7 says it is someone who was "pierced." Who was it that was pierced when he was nailed up to die? JESUS! But verse 8 says that it is Jehovah God who "is coming." Could it be there are two who are coming? No! Verse 8 refers to the ONE who is coming, not two. Revelation 1:8 states clearly that Jehovah God is the Alpha and the Omega.

Now note what he says at Revelation 22:12-13 (box 2). **"Look! I am coming quickly... I am the Alpha and the Omega, the first and the last..."** So Jehovah God is coming quickly. But notice the response when he says it again: **"Yes; I am coming quickly... Amen! Come Lord Jesus,"** (22:20, box 3).

Then again referring to the New World Translation, who is speaking in Revelation 2:8 (box 4)? **"These are the things that he says, 'the First and the Last,' who became dead and came to life again..."** Obviously that is Jesus, because the Father was never dead. (See also Revelation 1:17-18.)

> 1 7 LOOK! He is coming with the clouds, and every eye will see him, and those who pierced him; and all the tribes of the earth will beat themselves in grief because of him. Yes, Amen.
> 8 "I am the Al'pha and the O-me'ga," says Jehovah' God, "the One who is and who was and who is coming, the Almighty."

> 2 12 LOOK! I am coming quickly, and the reward I give is with me, to render to each one as his work is. 13 I am the Al'pha and the O-me'ga, the first and the last, the beginning and the end. 14 Happy are

> 3 20 He that bears witness of these things says, 'Yes; I am coming quickly.'" "Amen! Come, Lord Jesus."

> 4 8 And to the angel of the congregation in Smyr'na write: These are the things that he says, 'the First and the Last,' who became dead and came to life again. 9 'I know

Who is Jesus identifying himself as being when he called himself **"The First and the Last"**? This is how Almighty God described himself in the Old Testament. **"I am the first and the last; apart from me there is no God,"** (Isaiah 44:6). (see also Isaiah 48:11b & 12.)

Jesus is the **"Alpha and the Omega,"** the **"First and the Last"** - because Jesus is Jehovah God! No other conclusion is possible.

INFERIOR OR SUPERIOR TO WHOM?

Witnesses are taught to use John 14:28 to explain that Jesus is inferior to the Father. **"I am going to the Father, for My Father is greater than I."** Unfortunately the Witnesses have misunderstood that "greater" doesn't necessarily mean "better," and in this case it refers to position or order. An example is 1 Corinthians 11:3, where God speaks of His divine order. A husband is to be head over his wife as Christ is the head of the church. That isn't stating that husbands are better than wives, just different, for Galatians 3:28 says **"There is neither male nor female, for all are one in Christ."**

Another example of this divine order is Matthew 28:19, which list the Father, the Son and the Holy Spirit. This shows the order, and has nothing to do with importance or superiority. The vast majority of combined references in the New Testament are written in this same order.

Throughout the Bible we are told that worship of anyone or anything other than God is idolatry, for which serious judgement is the consequence. Revelation 22:8-9 commands there should be no worship of created beings such as angels, and this same message is also found in Colossians 2:18.

Hebrews 1:4 plainly states that Jesus Christ is "superior to" or "better than" the angels (depending on the version). In verse 6, Jehovah God Himself commands "Let all the angels of God worship Him (Jesus)." The New World Translation does split hairs with word differences such as "obeisance," but there can be no doubt about the meaning - Jesus is not the Archangel Michael, nor is He any other kind of angel. He must be God since the angels are commanded to worship Him. Any other conclusion involves false worship and the charge of idolatry, **"For**

THE ATTRIBUTES OF GOD

ATTRIBUTE	GOD THE FATHER	GOD THE SON	GODTHEHOLYSPIRIT
Eternal	Psalm 90:2	John 1:1	Hebrews 9:14
Omnipotent	1 Peter 1:5	2 Corinth. 12:9	Romans 15:19
(all powerful)	Matt. 19:26	Phil.3:21	1 Corinth. 12:8-11
Omniscient	Jeremiah 17:10	Revelation 2:23	1 Corinth. 2:10-11
(all knowing)		Coloss. 2:3	
Omnipresent	Jeremiah 23:24	Matthew 18:20	Psalm 139:7
(present everywhere)			Hebrews 9:14
Holiness	Revelation 15:4	Acts 3:14	Luke 1:15
Truth	John 7:28	Revelation 3:7	1 John 5:6

in Him (Jesus) dwells all the fullness of the Godhead bodily," (Colossians 2:9).

THE MYSTERY OF THE GODHEAD

The Bible teaches there is one God, who chooses to reveal Himself as three persons. 1 Timothy 3:16 describes this as "the mystery of the Godhead." God is so great and so awesome our puny little minds can barely grasp it. As the Bible states - **"His ways are higher than ours, and His thoughts are not our thoughts."**

Having said that, God has provided enough pointers in His Word to show this teaching about One God in three persons is true. The doctrine of the Godhead comes from the Bible. This was not invented by one of the councils of the Roman Catholic Church, contrary to the false and dishonest teachings of the Watchtower and some other cult groups. The facts are that Iraneus, Justin Martyr, Theophilus, Athenagorus, Tertullian, Origen and many other early Christian leaders reaffirmed the Bible teaching about the deity of Christ in their writings during the first two centuries.

Many have tried to explain the Bible doctrine called "The Trinity." St.

Patrick used a three-leafed clover, one leaf with three sections. Someone else used the illustration of a business firm, Smith, Brown & Jones - one firm with three partners. There is even the Triple-Point experiment from high school physics where water, H^2O, is put in a vacuum and the temperature lowered to zero, and at that precise moment you have solid ice, steam vapor and also liquid water. That is three forms of the most plentiful substance on earth at the same instant. Another illustration I have heard is the sun. The power of the combustion of the sun relates to the Father, and the light we see represents Jesus, the Son, while the heat we feel on our faces represents the effect of the Holy Spirit. On a hot day, if you put two saucers outside in the sun, one with butter, the other with cheese, you'll see the effect of our hearts: the butter will melt (representing a heart soft to the LORD), while the cheese will dry out and crack (representing a heart hardened to the LORD).

The Bible teaches and Christians believe in a God who has chosen to reveal Himself to mankind as Father-Son-Spirit. Unitarians cannot imagine this "Three-in-oneness" and so ridicule this doctrine because they cannot understand it. They fall back on simple arithmetic with the formula that $1 + 1 + 1 = 3$. The answer would be correct if the sum were correct, but unfortunately, the sum is wrong! The Bible never states and Christians do not believe that the Father plus the Son plus the Spirit add up to GOD.

It might be nearer the truth to set out the sum as follows, $1 \times 1 \times 1 = 1$. We are not asked to believe that the Trinity sets out the number of gods, but rather the greatness ("Greatness" = "dimensions" of "magnitude") of God. But mathematically speaking, the true equation should use the symbol for infinity, as follows:

$$\infty \times \infty \times \infty = \infty$$
$$(\infty = \text{infinity sign})$$

Most people have no problem about the reality of compound unity in secular life. In general terms most people accept the theory that our universe can be described in threefold unity as consisting of Space, Time and Matter. Space in turn is described in three directions as length, breadth and height. Time is perceived as past, present and future. Matter is described as energy, motion and phenomena.

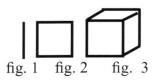

fig. 1   fig. 2   fig. 3

While on the subject of mathematics, let us note the following diagrams. Fig. 1 is an absolute Unity, of one dimension only. Fig. 2 is of two dimensions, but still is one object, not two separate units. Fig. 3 is a cube of three dimensions, a complete object with six facets, each of which could be a different colour to add beauty to its form, with almost infinite variety! Yet it is still one object, not three and its three-dimensional form of compound unity sets it in an entirely different category from Fig. 1 which in its absolute unity is incapable of beauty, variety or greatness!

Strangely enough, most people have no problem about the reality of compound unity in secular life. In general terms most people accept the theory that our universe can be described in threefold unity as consisting of Space, Time and Matter. Space in turn is described in three directions as length, breadth and height. Time is perceived as past, present and future. Matter is described as energy, motion and phenomena.

Now let us take another type of illustration, commonplace things in our daily lives, things that are known and experienced through our bodily senses. The first is the substance known as water.

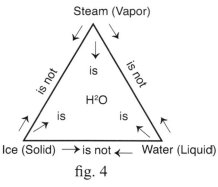

fig. 4

Fig.4. In the centre of the triangle we notice that the chemical formula is H_2O. H_2O is known to us all in three forms, as ice (solid), water (liquid), steam (vapour). Following the outside of the diagram we note that solid is not liquid and liquid is not vapour, but on the inside of the triangle, solid is H_2O and liquid is H_2O and vapour is H_2O. A threefold unity.

Fig. 5. The triangle this time represents electric waves, which are invisible yet known to us through our senses of sight, hearing and

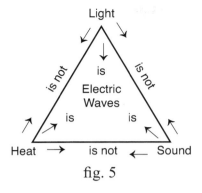

fig. 5

touch, as light, sound and heat. In daily life, to the non-scientist layman, they are three separate entities. Light is not heat and heat is not sound yet on the inner side of the diagram, we see that light is electric waves and heat is electric waves and sound is electric waves. This may be incompatible with reason, but to the scientist it is a proven fact of compound unity.

Fig. 6. Again we use the same diagram but with a very different purpose. We now deal with something beyond the range of our senses. The diagram represents "GOD" while the outer perimeter shows three points called "Father," "Son," and "Spirit." The Father is not the Son and the Son is not the Spirit but on the inner side we see that the Father is God, the Son is God, the Holy Spirit is God. Once again we find a perfect pattern of Compound unity or Trinity.

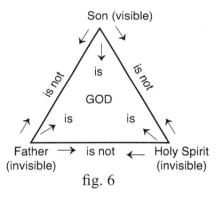

fig. 6

Man, stated in Scripture as being made in the image and likeness of God can be described as the sum of physical, mental and spiritual "components." A person may have a strong body, but be brain-dead clinically; is he truly Man? He may have both mental and physical wholeness but the moment the spirit leaves the body he becomes a corpse. Only as all three "components" function as a unity is he truly Man.

Surely, this threefold unity which pervades Creation at all levels from the vastness of space to the minuteness of the atom (one atom consists of protons, neutron, electrons) suggests that the entire plan of God in Creation and Revelation displays the truth that the Works of God reveal the Nature of God!

These can only give us a limited idea of the nature of God. I believe God would have us accept His word on faith.

Here are some Scriptures which prove the point.
"In the beginning <u>God</u> created..." (Genesis 1:1). The word for "God" here and elsewhere is Elohim, meaning God in the sense of plural or composite unity.

"Then God said, "Let <u>us</u> make man in <u>our</u> image, according to <u>our</u> likeness..." (Genesis 1:26).

"So God created man in <u>His own</u> image..." (verse 27).

"Come let <u>us</u> go down and confuse their language... so <u>the LORD</u> scattered them..." (Genesis 11:7,8).

What we see here is God speaking of Himself in the plural or composite unity of more than one person. There are two pertinent terms used in Hebrew to explain this. The first is YACHID, one absolute singular; and the other is ECHAD, one composite unity. Some further illustrations of this will help.

* In Genesis 2:24 Adam and Eve are described as one flesh. They don't become one person, but experience the mystery of 'one flesh' together.

* Numbers 13:23 speaks of a single cluster of grapes brought back by the spies for Moses. This cluster was so large it required two men to carry it, yet it is described as one in origin.

* Ezra 2:64 speaks of a whole assembly or group of people who were going to return from the captivity. They numbered 42,360 people yet they were one group. Ezra 3:1 says **"The people gathered together as one man."** The group of people didn't mutate into one person, but were united in purpose. All of these illustrations use the term Echad, one composite unity. Whenever the Bible speaks of God as One, it is always as Echad - not one singular solitary number but one undivided and indivisible essence with three eternal distinctions.

Consider the following;

THE FATHER	THE SON	HOLY SPIRIT	GOD
WHO RAISED JESUS FROM THE DEAD?			
Romans 6:4	John 2:19-21	Romans 8:11	Heb. 13:20
Acts 3:26	John 10:17,18		Acts 13:30
1 Thess. 1:10			Acts 17:31
WHO DOES THE BIBLE SAY GOD IS?			
Ephesians 4:6	Titus 2:13	Acts 5:3,4	Deut. 4:35
	John 1:1		
WHO CREATED THE WORLD?			
John 14:2	Coloss. 1:16,17	Genesis 1:2	Genesis 1:1
Exodus 20:11	John 1:1-3	Psalm 104:30	Heb.11:3
WHO SAVES AND REGENERATES MAN?			
1 Peter 1:3	John 5:21	John 3:6	1 John 3:9
	John 4:14	Titus 3:5	
WHO JUSTIFIES MAN?			
Jeremiah 23:6	Romans 5:9	1 Corinth. 6:11	Romans 4:6
2 Corinth. 5:19	2 Corinth. 5:19,21	Galatians 5:5	Romans 9:33
WHO SANCTIFIES MAN?			
Jude 1	Titus 2:14	1 Peter 1:2	Ex. 31:13

Some examples of these three distinctions are;

* When Jesus was baptized the Father spoke from heaven, while the Holy Spirit came down onto Jesus as He arose from the water, (Matthew 3:16-17). We are commanded to be baptized into three names of One God, in Matthew 28:19. There is no reason for Jesus and the Holy Spirit to be mentioned unless they are part of the One True God.

* **"For through Him (Jesus) we both have access by one (Holy) Spirit to the Father,"** (Ephesians 2:18). **"For there are three who bear witness in heaven: the Father, the Word, and the Holy Spirit;**

and these three are one," (1 John 5:7). If the Holy Spirit were just the power from the Father, then He wouldn't get a mention in the above Scriptures.

There is a point in time's distant past when no created beings existed. If God was singular (the Hebrew word is El) then there would be no love. But God is Elohim - plural - so He has never been alone. Love has always been present because love can only exist in the context of a relationship. That is why God is Love! I accept, by faith, the Bible's description of one God who shows Himself in three persons, because He said it.

Part of the problem the Watchtower and other cults suffer from is their inability to distinguish between the three classifications or groups of Scripture which concern Jesus Christ. These classifications were recognized by Aurelius Augustine sometime about 400AD.

First are those passages which *"teach the inferiority of Christ because He voluntarily became incarnate, was born as a baby, grew as a child, hungered, thirsted, grew tired, slept soundly and suffered every temptation common to man. In this truly human condition the Father was greater than He, and He constantly sought the leading of the Father,"*[27] according to Professor Gordon Lewis. Some examples of this are John 5:19, 8:42, 14:38, 16:28, Luke 2:40 and Mark 13:32.

The second group of Scriptures affirms that Jesus was distinct from the Father prior to any work of creation. *"He is distinguishable as a Word from the speaker of the word (John 1:1); as a uniquely begotten Son from His Father (John 1:14); as one who had priority not in time but in rank over all created things (Colossians 1:15, Revelation 3:14); as the shining is distinguishable from the sun, and as a perfect image is distinguishable from that which it portrays (Hebrews 1:3). In view of such passages the doctrine of the Trinity states that the Father and the Son are eternally distinct as persons. In this respect the Bible regularly recognises an order, placing the Father first, the Son second and the Holy Spirit third."*[27]

The third group of Scriptures teach us that the Father and the Son are not two separate beings or Gods, but rather one essence and spiritual substance. In this respect the Son is equally God. This clearly shows *"the Godhead is one in respect to essence, three in respect to personal distinctions, and three in respect to roles in the creative and redemptive programmes."*[27] Some examples of this grouping of Scriptures include John 1:1, 14, 20:28, Romans 9:5, and 1 John 5:20.

In summary, the Bible says there are three persons called God, and also that there is one God. There is only one possible conclusion; things equal to the same are equal to each other, therefore the three persons are One God, (Deuteronomy 6:4 & 1 John 5:7).

Should You Speak With Jehovah's Witnesses?
Some Christians use 2 John 10,11 to be rude and unresponsive to Jehovah's Witnesses. It reads:

"If anyone comes to you and does not bring this teaching, do not receive him into your house, and do not give him a greeting; for the one who gives him a greeting participates in his evil deeds."

However, this scripture, in context is not referring to the unsaved Jehovah's Witness at your door who has been deceived by the Watchtower Society. To understand the context we must look to the previous verses. Notice in verse 1 of 2 John, that this epistle is written to believers. Verse 7 begins, **"For many deceivers have gone out into the world..."** Gone out from where? Obviously from the congregation of believers to whom this letter is written. Verse 9 identifies them further as **"Anyone who goes too far and does not abide in the teaching of Christ..."**

This description could well apply to the early leadership of Jehovah's Witnesses who left the historic Christian Church, adopted the Arian heresy, and did not abide in the Biblical teaching of Christ. Their followers, however, usually the ones at your door, do not fit into this category of "Deceivers." They are not deliberately misrepresenting Christ, but are thoroughly deceived by their leaders.

The Jesus Of The Jehovah's Witnesses

Jehovah's Witnesses deny the Trinity, deny that Jesus is or ever was Almighty God, and reduce Him to the Archangel Michael in the heavens, only a good man on earth, and again Michael in the heavens after his resurrection. They admit that Jesus is "a god," but not the God. It is these issues that are addressed in the video, *"The Witness at Your Door."* Admittedly, these issues are dealt with briefly, but usually raise enough questions in the mind of the J.W.'s, that they begin to research on their own. Often they begin to examine scriptures in a recognized translation rather than their altered one, *"The New World Translation."*

Remember, we as Christians are to bear witness for Christ. We do not have to do the work of the Holy Spirit, that of convicting people of their sin. God will look after that, if we are faithful to let Him. I believe our instructions on witnessing are summed up very nicely in 2 Timothy 2:24-26:

"And the Lord's bond-servant must not be quarrelsome, but be kind to all, able to teach, patient when wronged, with gentleness correcting those who are in opposition, if perhaps God may grant them repentance leading to the knowledge of the truth, and they may come to their senses and escape from the snare of the devil, having been held captive by him to do his will."

Remember To Pray

Do not attempt to pray with the J.W., but pray ahead of time for the next two who will come. If they surprise you, excuse yourself for a few moments and pray before you speak with them. Remember, you must fight spiritual battles with spiritual weapons. It is good to take your authority in Jesus' name and bind the spirit of deception operating in their lives, and ask God to help you to say the right things to set them free. Then prepare yourself with a few timely scriptural points.

IF YOU ARE THINKING OF JOINING THE WATCHTOWER ... PLEASE COUNT THE COST FIRST!

You will be forced to give up the right to vote, to have holidays, including Christmas, etc., to have birthdays, to do military service (unless you live in Mexico), or even to smoke if you want to. These are all grounds for "disfellowshipping," or expulsion. Any family members who join the Watchtower organization will not be permitted to speak with you again. You could lose your family and friends, and even your livelihood. Doesn't it make you curious that Witnesses were permitted to do all of the above when Pastor Russell was the president?

Children will be discouraged from competitive sports, any kind of higher education (they might learn to think for themselves), most school and community activities and hobbies, in fact anything which fills your time so you can't be out selling Watchtower literature door to door. Most importantly, you will have to give up the right to think for yourself. You will be forced to hand over your mind in blind obedience to the Watchtower Leadership, whose honesty and integrity have been challenged by the hundreds of thousands who have left disillusioned.

MIND CONTROL

Cult groups such as the Watchtower, Moonies, Mormons, Christadelphians and many others utilize mind control methods to retain the support of people who would otherwise see through the serious flaws in the beliefs and history of that cult. "Mind Control, also called 'thought reform,' is more subtle and sophisticated [than brainwashing]. Its perpetrators are regarded as friends and peers, so the person is much less defensive... Mind control involves little or no overt physical abuse. Instead, hypnotic processes are combined with group dynamics to create a potent indoctrination effect. The individual is deceived and manipulated - not directly threatened - into making the prescribed choices. On the whole, he responds positively to what is done to him,"30 according to author and mind control expert, Steven Hassan. Hassan describes four main aspects of mind control.

Emotional Control includes the use of phobias, or bringing various fears and guilt onto a person. Daring to question the organization, or leaving it, will result in some horrible disaster happening to you, such as death etc. Such manipulation is usually subtle, but still very real.

Behavior Control occurs when socialising and entertainment are frowned on and replaced by meetings and "official" activities such as door to door work, (in many cases these are setups for rejection). Cult members are made to feel both special yet persecuted for their beliefs.

Thought Control involves a special language which is usually unique to that cult group. An example would be the Watchtower's use of terms such as "Theocratic," "God's Organization" and "Apostate," and so on. These and similar terms are used in a way to stop members thinking for themselves and to make them adopt the "official" thought patterns. These make the member believe that the organisation alone has all the answers and are custodians of "The Truth," while everything else is evil.

Information Control means that anything remotely critical of the organization is kept from the members. The leaders may be reading it so they can develop ways to counter what has been written, etc. Most cults are hierarchical or pyramidic in structure, so the higher you go, the more information you are permitted to access. How many ordinary members are told the full truth of the group's finances, or scandals involving the leaders? I've seen details where the Mormon Church bought a radio station in America and sacked all its staff after the station had broadcast details of homosexual activities of one of the top Mormon leaders. Ordinary members would have been excommunicated, but the leader was protected and attempts were made to hush the whole story up, it seems.

Cults like the Watchtower believe that the ends justifies the means; making you into a convert is more important than telling you the truth. Since they claim to be the only organization with the answers to all of life's problems, cult leaders shrewdly keep from converts the whole picture of what they are about, only drip-feeding information on a "need to know" basis. If members and prospective members were permitted to see the big picture, most would object to the indoctrination programme and probably leave.

Anecdotal (as well as an increasing amount of scientific and medical) evidence reveals a marked increase in emotional and mental disorders (such as schizophrenia) and family break-ups/child custody disputes with people involved with cult groups such as the Watchtower. We have already established from the Bible that salvation is not available in the Watchtower. If the real fruit of involvement in this organization is guilt and fear, growing into emotional disorders and family bust-ups, then I must ask what is the point in getting involved in such a group? It is my strong recommendation that people stay away from organisations such as the Watchtower, for the sake of their spiritual, mental and physical health, and turn instead to Jesus Christ, who is Savior, Lord, Counsellor and Friend.

POSSIBILITIES & CONSEQUENCES
Think about this for a moment. There really are only three main possibilities regarding the Watchtower Society - The Jehovah's Witnesses.

Possibility 1. It is possible both the Jehovah's Witnesses and the Christian Church, while sincere, are wrong about the truth. Both would then be false religions.

Possibility 2. It is possible the Jehovah's Witnesses are right about the truth. If the Witnesses are proclaiming the truth, then the Christian Church is wrong and is an apostate faith.

Possibility 3. It is possible the Christian Church is right about the Truth, and that the Jehovah's Witnesses are wrong. This would mean that the historic Christian faith is the true Gospel, and that the Jehovah's Witnesses are an apostate faith.

No one who has studied these issues can pretend Christianity and the Jehovah's Witnesses are even similar - many of their doctrines are poles apart.

What are the implications of these three possibilities?

If Possibility 1 is correct, then both the Jehovah's Witnesses and the Christian Church are wrong. Perhaps the Hindus have the truth, or Islam, or Mormonism, or even the Atheist! We need to explore all avenues which might lead to the Truth.

If Possibility 2 is correct, then the Christian Church is wrong and the Jehovah's Witnesses are right. This means that those who die prior to Armageddon will be resurrected into a perfect new body, and be "retrained" on a restored earth. They will have 1000 years to get it right, under the supervision of Jehovah's Witnesses. Even people like Hitler and Stalin will be included. Those who are still alive but outside the Jehovah's Witnesses at the time of Armageddon, including the unrepentant sinful, will sleep in their graves and be totally unaware of anything. They will depart into "everlasting cutting off" or instant annihilation, and so will escape eternal punishment. Such will rest in nonexistence. The best hope for those not wishing to belong to the Jehovah's Witnesses is to die prior to Armageddon, whenever that is. While still a gamble, eternal punishment is avoided.

If Possibility 3 is correct, that the Christian Church is right, and the Jehovah's Witnesses are wrong, and there is a heaven and a hell; then nothing good is in store for anyone losing this choice. Only true followers of Jesus Christ will be permitted to spend eternity with Him, (Hebrews 12:23; John 3:16-21; Rev. 2:11; 20:6).

Hell is for unbelievers and the rebellious, (Matthew 8:12; 25:41-46; Rev. 22:15). It is eternal separation from God in a painful, final and everlasting state, (Rev. 14:10-11; 2 Thess. 1:9).

The J.W. reference book, *"Reasoning From the Scriptures,"* (page 169) states *"There is no part of man that lives on when the body dies."* While Christians disagree, if this statement is Jehovah God's truth, then Jehovah's Witnesses (yes, even the 144,000) will not be resurrected or rewarded after their deaths. They also will experience annihilation.

God our Creator loves His creation, including you. He also sets the rules for Eternal Life. Are you prepared to gamble that the Jehovah's Witnesses have got it right, when they cannot get a single prophecy correct? Are you prepared to gamble that, despite its human imperfections, the Christian Church has got things so wrong? The answer is in Jesus Christ, not a religious organization! What are you now going to do about your eternal life? Choose your God carefully, for you will spend eternity with him.

WINNING WITNESSES TO CHRIST [31]

Jesus died for Jehovah's Witnesses as He did for all mankind. There are ways you can witness to cult members effectively. After all, about one million Witnesses have left in recent years, many through finding out that Jesus really is God. Witnesses are taught, at least twice a week, how to refute any argument you might present them. They are good at arguing. Their strength is in doctrine, even if it is false doctrine. You could play Scripture ping-pong until you drop from exhaustion. Most Christians who know their Bibles well could win arguments with Witnesses, but what does that prove? Winning an argument still doesn't get that person saved!

So how should we witness to them? If you have an effective method which works for you, don't change it - keep on with it, and let other Christians know about it. There are three main methods which people use with some success with Jehovah's Witnesses at their door.

* The first method involves doctrine. That means proving that Jesus is Jehovah God, the Godhead is a Trinity, Salvation is by grace and not by works, etc. While these things are true and while the Witness will have to learn these things at some stage, it takes a lot of time and intensive Bible study to try and learn this method. A lot of Christians don't have the time, resources or skills, although books like this should help, along with those by Ron Rhodes and Walter Martin listed on page 86.

* The second method is the historical method. This involves showing the Witness copies of their own literature which prove the Watchtower is a False Prophet and is inconsistent in its teaching. It is easy to show, for example, that the Watchtower Society has predicted the end of the world several times, and got it wrong several times. There is a list of

their major false prophecies near the beginning of this book. Probably the best two resources for this method are Randall Watters' and David Henke's books listed on page 86

Because of the mind control factor, Witnesses believe they have been told the truth by the Watchtower, despite the overwhelming evidence to the contrary. Have you ever tried to give a Witness a leaflet or book exposing their organization? That may be one of the quickest ways to get them to leave you alone, if that is what you want. They know the Watchtower forbids them to read anything which criticizes the organization, so it is "Apostate" literature. The reason for this is that Witnesses are actively discouraged (under penalty of being thrown out) from thinking for themselves. Total obedience to the official Watchtower teaching is obligatory.

* The third method could be called devotional. Experts in the cult field find this the most effective method, and I commend all Christians to learn this carefully. Jesus says the Gospel has to be so a child can understand it, so we have to aim at their hearts. Then God is released to do the work, and we don't have to strain. The best part about this method is you don't have to be a Bible scholar, and the Witness isn't prepared for it so they don't really know what to say, and it also avoids confrontation. This devotional method involves explaining to the Witness about sin and its consequences. Start with the Ten Commandments, explaining that while the ceremonial law was cancelled by Christ on Calvary, God's standard for a holy lifestyle remains consistent.

Get the Witness then to read you Matthew 5:21-48. Jesus here shows us that sin begins in the human heart. Murder, for example, is an outward expression of hatred, and God can see everything in our heart. We have to account for personal sins as well as all we inherited from Adam and our ancestors. The Witnesses can't fool themselves about being good. Ecclesiastes 7:20 says "There is not a just man on earth who does good and does not sin." God says that everybody sins. The penalty for our sin is death. Ecclesiastes 18:4 says "The soul that sins must die." So our sin means we are under God's wrath and judgement. These are sin. Lies theft, lust, murder, etc. (draw a wall - see example # 1.) So these are their sins, and this wall is between them and Jehovah

God. You cannot go over the wall, you can't go under it, you can't go around it, and you can't go through it. That is where you are, separated completely from God. He cannot hear you. There is only one way you can get to Jehovah God, and that is through Jesus Christ. Jesus is the bridge between you and God (see # 3). That is why Jesus is called Savior, because he came to save us from our sins (Matthew 1:21).

Turn now to Isaiah **"Behold, the Lord's hand is not shortened, that it cannot save, nor His ear heavy that it cannot hear. But your iniquities have separated you from your God; and your sins have hidden His face from you, so that He will not hear,"** (Isaiah 59:1-2). God can't hear you because of your sin. Isaiah 64:6 says "We are all like an unclean thing, and all our unrighteousness is like filthy rags." Tell the Witness that knocking on doors spreading their gospel and filling in their activities sheets isn't doing anything for them or their salvation. In fact in God's sight it is like filthy rags. That is how much He appreciates it when we are in our sin.

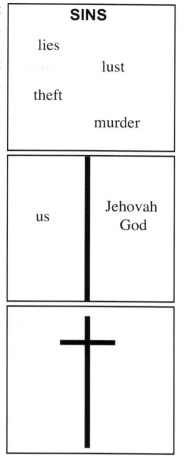

Explain what it cost Jesus. Get them to read John chapters 18 and 19. Jesus was falsely accused and received only the mockery of a trial. He was abandoned by His friends (Psalm 69:8) and rejected by almost everyone else (Psalm 41:9). He was scourged, whipped to within an inch of His life by a whip studded with lead and bones ripping at His back. His head was pierced by a crown of thorns. He was stripped, beaten, humiliated, spat on and then forced to carry His own cross, until the weight almost crushed Him. Then He was dragged up the hill at Golgotha and nailed with huge metal spikes onto the wood, and when the cross was dropped into the hole in the ground, many of his bones were knocked out of joint. He hung there through the greatest heat of the day.

If that wasn't enough, God heaped on Jesus all our sins, yours, mine, everyone's. The sight was so ghastly even God had to turn His back on His own Son (Isaiah 53). Carrying all of that tremendous burden, Jesus became the sacrificial Lamb of God. He took my place, just as He took your place too. Jesus is our High Priest, for He offered not the blood of animals but Himself as the full and final sacrifice for sin, (John 10:11-18 & Hebrews 9:12). Jesus is called Savior, because he came to save us from our sins (Matthew 1:21). Jesus did all this because He loves you and me. This shows His grace because we can never earn a pardon for our sins. However when we repent of all our sins and ask Jesus to come into our lives as our Lord and Savior, then His forgiveness is real and permanent.

Remember this: *"It wasn't the Romans who caused Jesus' death. It wasn't the Jews. It was sin! Jesus Christ died to take our sin, yours and mine, and if you were to die today, without repenting of your sin, it would be as though you were charged with the murder of Jesus Christ."*

Then give them your testimony. Tell them how you found peace in your heart, and assurance of salvation when you gave your life to Christ. Tell the Witness that when they stand before Jehovah God on the day of judgement, they will stand alone. They do not stand with the district circuit overseer, they do not stand with a presiding elder, and they do not stand as part of an organization. They stand alone, and are accountable for themselves. Then you can read them John 6: 35-37. Jesus said to them "I am the bread of life, he that comes to Me shall never hunger, and he that believes in Me will never thirst. All that the Father gives to Me will come to Me, and the one who comes to Me I will by no means cast out." Then tell the Witness the choice is theirs, they can come to an organisation or they can come to Jesus Christ, but only Jesus Christ provides true salvation. When they leave - pray for them. Get their names and keep praying for them for as long as it takes.

TESTIMONY OF "ANNE" - FORMER JEHOVAH'S WITNESS

I became involved in the Jehovah's Witnesses in 1981, and spent the next 18 months having weekly Bible studies and attending their Sunday meetings at the Kingdom Hall. I had actually been brought up a Catholic in the late 1950's and early 60's. In those days we were taught the catechism which is basic Catholic doctrine. I had always known about Adam & Eve and Jesus and the Ten Commandments, but I never stopped to think that these, or the epistles or the gospel which was read at mass were from the Bible, so my knowledge was extremely limited. When I was old enough to spread my wings I drifted away from church and only went to mass and confessions at Christmas and Easter. It was when I was married and my oldest child was turning five that I thought it was time I took the responsibility to give him and his sister a grounding in the faith so they could at least make some choices later on. I started going back to mass and I was made to feel so welcome by the padre and the local parishioners in the army camp where we were living at the time. I became involved in Christian doctrine classes for school-age kids, and I got roped in as a helper. I was in for quite a shock. Things had changed so much, the old grey catechism book had been replaced by the Bible. I remember meeting with another mother one afternoon to help prepare a lesson, and being asked to look up one of the Psalms. I was mortified - I didn't even know where to start. It was quite a relief when we were notified of a posting back to Upper Hutt (a city near the capital), not much later.

Once again I was roped into doing CCD, much against my will I might add. So I decided it was time I became familiar with this Bible business. I started reading Bible stories to my kids each bed-time, and of course we started right back in Genesis, and that was fine. However the further I went the more disturbed I became with some of the stories. The very last straw was when I read to the kids about Deborah and Barak, how she had killed Sicera as he slept by impaling him to his pillow with a stake, I couldn't believe it. A matter of days later two Jehovah's Witnesses arrived at my door, and wanted to show me something from the Bible. My immediate reaction was I don't want to know - the stories are disgusting. Of course that led to a discussion, and because I was really interested in Christian things it led to more and more questions. They seemed to be able to provide me with plausible answers.

Around this time the Springbok tour was on. I didn't think I would ever see riots like that in New Zealand. Our neighbour was a policeman, and a Maori. He and his family were receiving threatening phone calls. I was appalled at what was happening. It was happening all over the globe and here it was at my own back door. Again the Witnesses were able to tell me it was because we were in the end times. They were showing me verses of scripture to back up what they were saying. As I said originally it led to eighteen months of study and going to meetings. I had cut ties with the Catholic church, and that was no easy decision. I was actually at the point when I was seriously considering baptism as a Jehovah's Witness.

The reason I came out was by this stage my husband was very unhappy with my involvement. I had lots of head knowledge, but I was really screwed up inside, and very unhappy. The more anti (my husband) became, the more stubborn I was. I had been warned I would be persecuted for the sake of the Kingdom, and even though I was terribly miserable I couldn't let it go because I knew there was more to this Christianity thing than I had experienced before.

To cut a long story short I virtually backed him into a corner. He felt he could do nothing else but leave. Prior to this we had a good marriage so I was feeling absolutely desperate. I tried to make contact with the priest who had been in Waiouru - no luck. At that time I discovered 1 Corinthians 10:13 in my New World Translation. And I kept going back to it because it said "No temptation or trial comes upon us that is not common to man. God is faithful. He will not allow you to be tempted beyond what you can endure, and He will give you a way out." I just held onto that verse, and cried out to Jehovah for help.

The help came in the form of a phone call from an old friend who had become a born-again Christian. She wanted to visit. I was immediately on the defensive as I assumed someone had been gossiping. Jo and another friend Carol used to really bug me. They were both very vocal Christians, and what's more they were so much more enthusiastic and excited about their faith than I was. I used to deliberately keep out of their way. Anyway Jo arrived, and was no sooner in the door and the phone went. It was one of my husband's army mates. He was ringing to see if he could do anything to help. My husband at that stage had approached his boss about moving back into the barracks. Jo is a very direct, forthright person. I had no sooner hung up and she asked straight out if our marriage was on the rocks. Well, floodgates opened and she copped the whole lot. She spent that whole day (and it was a whole day) bombarding me with scripture counteracting anything I threw at her, which was really amazing as she was only a very new Christian herself. By the time she had left I had committed my life to Jesus, and decided to return all my books to my J .W. friends and to break off further studies.

That was extremely difficult, as they had been wonderful friends. They had been particularly supportive during a four month period when my husband had been overseas, and also when our son had been very ill. I knew my decision was going to upset them, and I knew I was going to lose their friendship as well. It was however a time of reconciliation for my husband and I, and we've not long celebrated our 21st Anniversary.

That wasn't the end of it though. It took months and months and months to overcome the indoctrination I had had. I committed my life four times to the Lord before I was truly convinced I was a Christian. I had lost credibility with myself, let alone anybody else. Even though I had accepted Jesus into my life, I kept it pretty much to myself for a very long time. That was difficult as I knew I should be witnessing to my faith, if I really meant business. I look back now and I am so grateful to God for His love, His tenderness, His patience and His guidance.

I encourage you to pray for the Witnesses who come to your door. Many of them like me have come out of a mainstream church. They usually have an incredible zeal for God. They know the importance of evangelism, especially friendship evangelism. If you can send them away with a doubt, with something to think about, just as Jo and Carol did by their attitude, is much more value than getting into a full-blown debate. The antagonism they often receive at the door only serves to reinforce in their minds that they are being persecuted for the sake of the Kingdom. The difference is they are trying to earn their way to God's Kingdom. But we have the liberty, we have the freedom, we have to assurance of our place in God's Kingdom. We have discovered that when we put Jesus in his rightful place, that is God's free gift to us. Please pray for them!"

RULES FOR JEHOVAH'S WITNESSES [32]

If you decide to join this organization there are rules for members - here are some which might interest you.

1. You cannot celebrate holidays such as Christmas, Easter, Thanksgiving, Mother's Day, Father's day or any other national holiday.

2. You must not take an oath of allegiance to your country, join the military, vote, or support any political party.

3. You can if you wish collect unemployment or welfare benefits. This is encouraged if possible because you will have more time to go door-to-door with their Society's magazines.

4. You cannot celebrate birthdays.

5. You cannot clink glasses together.

6. You cannot throw rice or confetti at weddings.

7. Large gatherings are frowned upon by the Watchtower Society unless organized by them for Bible studies. (Usually the Bible is not used much, their other books are claimed to be "better" to learn from.)

8. You must not associate socially with anyone not a Witness except to conduct a Bible (book) study.

9. Your children must not associate with other children unless they are Witnesses.

10. Your children cannot join organizations such as the Boy Scouts, Girl Guides, Red Cross, S.P.C.A, Boys or Girls clubs, team sports at school or elsewhere. Their time is considered better spent distributing the Society's magazines and books.

11. Adults may not join groups such as volunteer fire brigades, the YMCA etc. or service clubs, in order to avoid "worldly associations."

12. A minimum of 10 hours a month is encouraged for door-to-door selling of the Society's books and magazines on a contribution basis. Monthly reports must be filled in. (Jehovah God will apparently consult these to see if you are worthy to survive Armageddon.)

13. On public holidays you must still attend meetings and give out literature where possible.

14. You must not read any literature published by Christian churches or other religious organizations. These are claimed to be from Satan.

15. You must not acknowledge the Cross as a Christian symbol. It is considered to be of pagan origin.

16. Jehovah Witnesses provide no Sunday school for your children. You must provide four hours per month studying with them from the Watchtower Society's publications.

17. You must make sure you have time off from your job to attend all the Watchtower conventions, held three times a year. If you miss them you will be frowned upon.

18. There are certain rules of conduct to follow in your bedroom. You may check with the elders for more information. If you disobey you may be disfellowshipped (expelled).

19. Certain forms of birth control are unacceptable. This is not your decision, check with the elders first.

20. Beards are frowned upon as they reflect a rebellious and independent attitude. Moustaches are okay.

21. If your family members are not J.W.'s you must have little or nothing to do with them. If any have been expelled have NOTHING to do with them or you will be shunned too.

22. Make sure that all your magazine and book studies are done and underlined each week.

23. All meetings must be attended. There are only five per week, on three different days. If you don't attend you must have good reason. Sickness is NOT always a good reason.

24. You must view all people who are not J.W.'s as "worldly" and part of Satan's organization. They will all perish at Armageddon and only J.W.'s will be saved, so why bother associating with them?

25. If by chance after you join, you ever decide to leave, all your new "friends" will shun you, even if you are not "disfellowshipped." You will also get frequent calls of "encouragement" which may be viewed as harassment. If you were ever to attend a Christian church for any reason (including family weddings, funerals, etc.) you will be automatically disfellowshipped.

26. You must never disagree with the Society or it will be said that you are disagreeing with God, because the Watchtower Society claims to be the ONLY organisation on earth that has been chosen by Him to guide his people.

27. You will not have the free choice of conscience. You give up that right when you become a Witness. The Society will make almost all decisions for you.

28. You will be forbidden to give or take a blood transfusion or blood products. You must not even store your own blood for a transfusion as it is said this belongs to God. If your child requires a transfusion, it is your duty to try and prevent the doctors from transfusing the child even

it means stealing the child from the hospital and letting him or her die. 29. You may not partake of the bread and the wine during communion (or Eucharist), unless you are one of the 144,000 who are the only ones who may go to heaven.

30. All above rules are subject to change without notice and without recourse. Be in constant expectation of "New Light" which could reverse everything.

31. If you disobey any of the above rules, and refuse to turn around from your rebellious course, you will be disfellowshipped, and an announcement will be made to the whole congregation. All members worldwide will shun you, even family members, so expect no invitations to family weddings, funerals or reunions etc.

32. If you wish to be reinstated, you must do as the elders tell you: attend all meetings, coming in after the opening song and prayer, sitting at the back of the hall, talk to no one, have no participation, leave before the final song and prayer and have no contact with other members. You may have no part in field ministry until reinstated. Depending on your offence the time of punishment may last up to a year or more.

33. You must not pray for disfellowshipped ones. They are dead in God's eyes.

If this is the religion you want to be part of and you join it, expect to be very busy in activities sponsored by the Watchtower Society of Jehovah's Witnesses. If you can't keep up, expect to be plagued by guilt and fear for failing the Watchtower Society. In fact, several medical research studies over the past thirty years in Europe and North America show that serious mental and emotional problems among Jehovah's Witnesses are between ten and 16 times above the population averages.

Conclusion: The Watchtower Society is so easy to get into, and there is no honorable way out! Perhaps you should think very carefully before committing yourself to an organization like this.

To the Jehovah's Witness: A sincere faith misdirected away from the God of the Bible will not save you. Become a seeker of the truth about the real Jesus Christ.

To the Ex-Jehovah's Witness: We know you were told there is no hope or help for you outside the Watchtower Society. <u>They were wrong!</u> There are tens of thousands who have left the Watchtower and received help. Some are now available to help you, along with others who have studied this and similar cults. Please feel free to contact us, in confidence. Please don't give up on Jehovah God because of the errors of the Watchtower Society. We especially recommend that you renounce the false baptism you may have had because of the spiritual ties and bondages this brings on members.

To Christians & others who care: If you have a burden to reach Witnesses and inform the public about the real doctrines of The Watchtower, we need your help. We have materials to share. Many items are freely available from our website. All donations are used without personal gain. People deserve to have complete and accurate information before making decisions that will determine their eternal destiny!

(The above information reflects current teaching of the Watchtower Society at time of printing)

HOW TO PRAY EFFECTIVELY FOR WITNESSES

* The first matter to understand is that the battle is spiritual. Ephesians 6:12 says **"For we do not wrestle against flesh and blood (your relative/friend) but against principalities, against powers, against the rulers of darkness of this age, against spiritual hosts of wickedness in heavenly places."** We are not fighting your loved one. They are in spiritual bondage. We are going to deal with the demonic spirits which blind and deafen them to the truth of the Gospel of God, and which prevent them responding to Him.

* Make sure there is no unconfessed sin in your life. If so, put it right with God, and if possible with anyone else involved.

* Know your authority in Christ to overcome all the power of the evil one. **"I give you the authority to trample on serpents and scorpions (demons), and over all the power of the enemy, and nothing shall by any means hurt you. Nevertheless, do not rejoice in this, that the spirits are subject to you, but rather rejoice because your names are written in heaven,"** (Luke 10:19-20).

* If possible, ask another Christian believer to agree with you in prayer. **"...If two of you agree on earth concerning anything that they ask, it will be done for them by My Father in heaven,"** (Matthew 18:19). What if you are alone, and have no-one to agree with you? Lori MacGregor (a former cult member who now heads up a Christian ministry to reach people in cults) recommends you ask Jesus to agree with you. Then pray to God in the name of the Savior Jesus Christ as the Holy Spirit directs you.

* Bind the principal demonic strongman, "The Spirit of Watchtower Deception," in the name of Jesus Christ. **"Assuredly, I say to you, whatever you bind on earth will be bound in heaven..."**(Matthew 18:18). This is needed to restore the spiritual sight to people. 2 Corinthians 4:4 explains about evil spirits or demons which blind people to the truth. Jesus gives us the delegated authority to deal with those spirits, thereby releasing the person to make their own choices.

Other demonic spirits which need to be bound include; Antichrist, Unbelief, Error, False Doctrine, Confusion, Legalism, Hardness, Harshness, Guilt, Fear of Watchtower Authorities, Fear of Armageddon, etc. (Ask the Holy Spirit for the names or effects caused by these and other demonic spirits, and how to cut off their influence on your loved one.)

* Ask God to release and loose your relative/friend from these demonic spirits and all others which control them. **"...Whatever you loose on earth will be loosed in heaven,"** (Matthew 18:18). Let me explain the purpose of this. You are merely restoring a level playing field, spiritually. Your attitude should never be to control the person - that is what we are trying to set them free from! 2 Corinthians 4:4 explains about spirits which blind people spiritually. If you are in Christ - in relationship with Jesus - then you have delegated authority to bind those spirits so the person may have their will back.

* Ask the Lord to release your loved one's emotions, which have been held in fear and bondage for so long. The Holy Spirit will do this gently and lovingly, so that person comes to understand who they really are, and how much Jesus really loves them.

* Be assured that God is now at work in their lives to release them from their bondage. Pray for their salvation, in faith. If the person is a family member, God's promise to you is to **"Believe on the Lord Jesus Christ, and you shall be saved, you and your household,"** (Acts 16:31).

If they are not a family member, God provides another promise for you to appropriate in prayer for them. **"The Lord is not slack concerning His promise... but is longsuffering towards us, not willing that any should perish but that all should come to repentance,"** (2 Peter 3:9), and **"God our Savior... desires all men to be saved and to come to the knowledge of the truth,"** (1 Timothy, 2:4). God's Word is plain, He doesn't want your relative/friend in the Watchtower Society to perish, to be wiped out at Armageddon, or on Judgement Day. God wants them saved, and we have a commission from Him to do the job in prayer, and to find out how to share Jesus with them effectively.

* Keep on praying in faith for your loved one. Experience shows that perseverance produces the best results, so don't be discouraged if there are no positive signs for a while. Ask the Lord to make His word alive to them, to show them the truth, even from the corrupted New World (mis)Translation.

In the very second Witness "Bible Lesson" people are taught that the Devil will try to oppose their study of the Bible with them. When family and friends find out what the person is doing with the Witnesses, most people usually know it is wrong, even if they don't know why. If you jump up and down loudly condemning the Watchtower as cultic, the Witnesses will have been proved right, and your family member/ friend will be confirming this in their minds. You will be known as an "Opposer," and will have lost your right to speak on matters of religion etc. to your friend. It is highly likely you will be cut off, as though you were dead, and never permitted to communicate with them again.

Try very hard not to make statements, such as "Leave the Watchtower alone, they will screw your mind up," (even if it is true). Instead, try asking gentle questions so they think they are teaching you. They are being programmed not to listen to "criticism." For example, the material in this book is "Apostate,"according to the Watchtower Society, and because of the increasing mind-control used, your friend will soon know they are not permitted to read it. Trying to make them will only succeed in cutting you off as a friend. If you force them to make a choice between you and the Watchtower, or even the Bible and the Watchtower, they will almost always choose the Watchtower.

It is most important to prevent people studying with the Witnesses in the first place, because getting people out can take years and much heartache. Seek expert help as early as possible whenever a close friend or family member shows an interest in the Witnesses. Pray for God's wisdom, which He gives to those who seek Him. I was told by a former Witness they would never have joined the Watchtower if they had been shown this book early enough.

PRAYER OF RENUNCIATION & RELEASE

for those previously involved in the Watchtower Society/J. W.'s

(Please pause briefly following each paragraph to allow the Holy Spirit to show any additional issues which He may wish to bring to your attention)

"Father God, creator of the heavens and the earth, I come to you in the name of Jesus Christ your Son. I choose to accept the sacrifice made by Jesus at Calvary for me to pay for my sins and iniquities. I come as a sinner seeking forgiveness and cleansing from all sins I have committed against you, and against all others made in your image. I honour my earthly father and mother, and all of my ancestors of flesh and blood, and of the spirit by adoption, but I utterly turn away from and renounce all their sins. I forgive all in my family line for the effects of their sins on me and my children. I confess and renounce all of my own sins. I renounce and rebuke Satan and every power of his affecting me and my family.

In the name of the Lord Jesus Christ, I renounce every action and word of mine which gave others permission to deceive and control me. I renounce, forsake and break every covenant I have ever made with the Watchtower Society of Jehovah's Witnesses. I renounce and forsake the false headship and authority of the President and the Governing Body of the Watchtower Society, and their idolatrous usurping of their organization in the place of the Lord Jesus Christ.

In the name of Jesus Christ, I renounce and forsake the heretical writings of Charles Taze Russell, Joseph Rutherford, Nathan Knorr, Frederick Franz, Milton Henchel, and all other writings published by the Watchtower Society. Lord Jesus, help me to honour you by removing all these books and publications from my home and life, and I cut off every bondage I have been under because of those writings, in the name of Jesus Christ.

In the name of Jesus Christ I renounce and cut off my life the ungodly

Covenants of Baptism and Membership of the Jehovah's Witnesses; I renounce these and all other ungodly soul ties, and I command the spirits that empower those soul ties to leave me now in the name of Jesus Christ. I gather those soul ties together and sever them through with the Sword of the Spirit of God, and humbly request the blood of Jesus Christ to seal those ends so they will never be able to reconnect.

Holy Spirit, given by my savior Jesus Christ as my wonderful teacher, counsellor, and revealer of God's Word, (the Bible) I confess and apologise for accepting the false teaching and belief that you are not Deity but only the power of God like electricity. Please forgive me, and do not hold me guilty of the only unforgiveable sin, namely blaspheming the Holy Spirit, as stated by Jesus Christ and as shown in Matthew chapter 12 verses 31 & 32. You know all my problems, all those things which bind, torment, defile and harass me. I now confess that my body is the temple of the Holy Spirit, redeemed, cleansed and sanctified by the blood of Jesus Christ.

I ask you, Lord Jesus, to fill me now with your Holy Spirit, so that He will give me insight and understanding when I read and study your Word. I enthrone you, Lord Jesus in my heart, for you are my Lord and Saviour, the source of eternal life. Thank you, Father God, for your mercy, your forgiveness and your love, in the name of Jesus Christ. Amen."

If you have difficulty going through this prayer, then please contact the publishers listed on page 2 (Jubilee has links with ministries which can assist in most countries world-wide); or contact a competent Christian leader near you to assist you.

Find Bible-believing Christians and spend time with them. Please explain to them you are coming out of a deceptive cult and need their encouragement and support at least until you are firmly on your feet. If some disappoint you (probably through not understanding your need) don't be put off, for there are caring Christians around who can and will help.

LETTER OF RESIGNATION

If you have ever become a member of the Jehovah's Witnesses (Watchtower Bible & Tract Society) or been baptized by them, it is important that you send a letter of resignation. I suggest you send your letter to the national office of your country, and a copy to the world headquarters. You could also send a copy to your local Kingdom Hall elders. They also need to know about the real Jesus Christ.

Try to use your own words in your letter, but to assist you below is a sample you could use. If you wish to use our suggestion, please scroll over the text and copy onto a blank piece of paper.

You may care to mention you have discovered that Jesus is Jehovah God; that you are now certain of your salvation; that the Watchtower Society and publications had misled you because they contained false prophecies and doctrines; and you can no longer accept the polytheism the Watchtower teaches.

If you are or were a member of Watchtower Society of Jehovah's Witnesses, and wish to formally resign, we suggest you scroll over the text and copy onto a blank piece of paper, complete the relevant sections and send one copy to your local, National & International H.Q. in New York USA.

(This is also available on our website for free download. Look for Free Stuff)

RESIGNATION FROM

The Watchtower Society of Jehovah's Witnesses

Local Church...
National HQ..
International HQ, 900 Red Mills Road, Wallkill NY 12589-3223, USA

To the Presiding Overseer, Sir:

I have been studying to prove the invitation by Joseph Rutherford are true, where he said, *"If the message Jehovah's Witnesses are bringing to the people is true, then it is of the greatest importance to mankind.*

If it is false then it is the duty of the clergymen and others who support them to come boldly forward and plainly tell the people wherein the message is false," (The Golden Age, Joseph Rutherford, p. 252).

Like a good Berean, as mentioned in the Bible, I have discovered the following:

Contrary to the Bible, the "Jesus" of the Watchtower Society of Jehovah's Witnesses is Michael the archangel, the first and greatest creation of Jehovah God. You claim Michael came to earth and lived as a man, got himself killed (which was pointless) and rose as a spirit. He invisibly returned to earth in 1914 when you claim the Millennium began, and established his headquarters in Brooklyn, New York.

I have discovered that Jesus Christ is fully God (1 Timothy 3:16). Jesus Christ was never Michael, because Daniel 10:13 says, "... **Michael, ONE of the chief princes...**" meaning that Michael is not unique at all but merely one of several. Are we to assume then that there are many Christs, of which Jesus is one? That's ridiculous! You teach that Jude 9 refers to Christ, although Michael is plainly identified as an Archangel (or "chief of the Angels"). The context shows that Michael did not dare rebuke Satan. Jesus, on the other hand, repeatedly rebuked Satan (Matthew 17:18; Mark 9:25, etc.). Further, Hebrews 1:6 commands all the angels to worship Jesus. God the Father would hardly command angels to worship another angel. That would be idolatry, and cause for serious condemnation.

The Watchtower Society of Jehovah's Witnesses denial of the deity of Jesus sadly means that they have no assurance of salvation, because they reject the very source of that salvation. I have discovered the Watchtower Society of Jehovah's Witnesses has adopted the heresy of Arius, which has no Biblical support. Jesus Christ did NOT return to Earth in 1914, as claimed by the Watchtower Society, and He is never going to sneak back unseen, according to Revelation 1:7.

Because Jesus Christ has become my mediator between me and the Heavenly Father, according to Acts 7:59, 1 Corinthians 1:2, & 1

Timothy 2:5, I can and should pray to Jesus Christ, contrary to the teachings of the Watchtower Society of Jehovah's Witnesses.

The New World Translation used by the Watchtower Society of Jehovah's Witnesses was translated by a known spiritist, Johannes Greber, and therefore cannot be regarded as the reliable Word of God.

I have also discovered that the Watchtower Society of Jehovah's Witnesses has made many prophetic announcements, but according to Deuteronomy 13: 1-8; 18:20-22; Jeremiah 23:40, & 2 Peter 1:20-21, the Watchtower Society has failed the Biblical tests to be a Prophet from God. Consequently I am left with the clear and unequivocal conclusion the Watchtower is a false prophet.

So my questions to honest and thinking Watchtower Society of Jehovah's Witnesses are these:

How do you know that what you are told to be true today won't be declared false tomorrow?
Or what you are told is false today won't be declared true tomorrow?

The Bible is very clear that God cannot lie (1 Samuel 15;29 & Romans 3:4) and that He is unchanging and unchangeable (Malachi 3:6 & James 1:17). God is not the author of confusion (1 Corinthians 14:33). It is clear that the *"spiritual enlightenment"* claimed by the Leaders of the Watchtower Society of Jehovah's Witnesses cannot have come from God. The source of their confusion is either soulish, or inspired by Satan himself. It does show that anyone who chooses to get involved with the Watchtower does so at the risk of deception. Spiritual truth is never based on someone's testimony, but on the objective Word of God, the Bible. It isn't what we think that really matters - it is what God says in the Bible.

I renounce my association with and all my obligations to the Watchtower Society of Jehovah's Witnesses, without the least equivocation, mental reservation, or self-evasion of mind. For the Word of God says: **"Do not be unequally yoked together with unbelievers. For what fellowship has righteousness with lawlessness? And what communion has light with darkness?"** (2 Corinthians 6:14).

I have no animosity towards you personally, nor any other church member I trust you did not seek to deceive me deliberately, but the teachings of Watchtower Society of Jehovah's Witnesses had deceived us both.

I request that you formally acknowledge this resignation in writing as soon as possible.

Respectfully,

Name...

Address..

Date...

SUMMARY

In summary the Jehovah's Witnesses are a religious group who are out of step with the Bible. They also meet the definitions of a cult. Essentially the Watchtower Society seems to be a commercial organisation, geared to make money from magazine and book sales. The wealth so created is not shared with the members. Despite over one million leaving the Watchtower Society over the past two decades, this cult continues to reject many Christian teaching from the Bible, despite using Bible terminology. Their track record of false prophecies and changing doctrines at whim is unrivalled among cults. Their "New World Translation" of the Bible is unanimously rejected by reputable scholars and theologians. The Watchtower denial of the deity of Jesus sadly means that Jehovah's Witnesses have no assurance of salvation, because they reject the very source of that salvation. The people the Watchtower send to knock on our doors have undergone a form of mind-control and need to know they have been deceived. They especially need the love of Christians and to hear the reason for our faith in the God of the Bible. Because the Watchtower is one of the most man-made cults on earth we should work and pray to set free in Christ those the Watchtower hold in bondage. Let Jesus, the true God of love, shine through you.

NAMES OF KNOWN WATCHTOWER BREAKAWAY GROUPS OR FRONT ORGANIZATIONS;

Ambassadors for Christ	Bible Students Assn..
Bible Studies Fellowship	Bible Way Publications
Christian Millennial Fellowship	Christian Renewal Ministries
Church of God-Faith of Abraham	Dawn Bible Students
Faithbuilders Fellowship	Laodicean Home Missionaries
Laymans Home Missionary Movement	Standfast Movement

Appendix

Pagan Roots Of Jehovah's Witnesses Found In Their History

(This was written by Lorri MacGregor of Canada, who was a Jehovah;s Witnesses for 15 years, before coming to the knowledge that she had been deceived and discovered the true Jesus Christ and His nature.)

The Watchtower of July 15, 1950, page 212 make the following revealing statement about their founder,

"In his teens Charles Taze Russell, the editor, had been a member of the Congregational Church and a strong believer in the eternal torture of damned human souls in a hell of literal fire and brimstone... But when trying to reclaim an acquaintance, an infidel, to Christianity, he himself was routed from his sectarian position and driven into scepticism. Hungrily he began investigating the heathen religions in search of the truth on God's purpose and man's destiny. Proving all these religions unsatisfactory and before giving up religious investigation altogether, he took up the search of the Holy Scriptures from a sceptic's viewpoint, now untrammelled by the false religious doctrines of the sectarian systems of Christendom."

What an admission! He knew so little of the Christian faith and what the Bible taught, that an "infidel" drove him into scepticism. Not only that, he filled his mind with pagan, occult beliefs before returning as an obviously last choice to the Bible.

Notice his approach to the Holy Scriptures was as a "sceptic," not a believer, feeling he was free from the influence of "Christendom." I'll say he was! His mind was not protected by sound doctrine, and his head was full of the pagan, occult teaching he had so eagerly sought. It will become more and more apparent as we pursue the pagan roots of the Jehovah's Witnesses that he retained that pagan influence, all the while professing to be an unspotted Christian.

Readers of the very first issue of "Zion's Watch Tower" should have alerted his followers to his intentions to fuse the occult with Christianity when he stated,

" a truth presented by Satan himself is just as true as a truth stated by God"... and "...accept truth wherever you find it. "

In his personal life he was greatly influenced by a prevailing health treatment. Various psychics professed to give "readings" by examining the bumps on one's head. This is certainly not a Christian practice, and in fact, leaves one open for spiritistic influence.

He was already supposed to be dispensing Bible truth when he was, at the same time, obviously concerned with the shape of one's skull. During this time he taught in the Watchtower Magazines of March 15, 1913 and January 15th, 1912, that one's desire to worship God was due to the shape of one's brain. He also felt that if a dog's head was shaped like a man's, the dog would think as a man! Phrenology is not Christianity, yet he attempted to fuse the two beliefs.

Pagan Symbols On Watchtower Publications

If one examines Russell's theology in his series of books called *"Studies in the Scriptures"* he will notice a blatantly occult symbol adorning the covers. The winged solar disk is a symbol of ancient Egypt representing the sun god. Throughout the centuries it came to represent various other pagan deities. It was, in fact, the symbol for the Baal gods during Jezebel's time. Russell attempted to fuse paganism and Christianity and pass it off as untainted Christianity.

It's interesting that even the Watchtower Society admits that it was a fear of hellfire that drove young Charles Russell to seek an alternative faith. Although the Society denied writing a biography of their founder (see Jehovah's Witnesses in the Divine Purpose, page 63), they, in fact, wrote three, in 1925, 1926, and 1927.

The Watchtower Society has a history of lying, not only to outsiders, but to its own members! Is this Christian or Pagan? The Society tries to make it Christian by calling it "justified lying." This doctrine is still in place down to our day.

We have just considered an example where they denied writing a biography of Charles Russell, but really wrote three. This doesn't fit their definition of "justified lying" which is also called "theocratic war strategy." Justified lying is defined by them as follows:

"As a soldier of Christ he is in theocratic warfare and he must exercise added caution when dealing with God's foes. Thus the Scriptures show that for the purpose of protecting the interests of God's cause, it is proper to hide the truth from God's enemies..." (Watchtower, June 1/60 p. 352).

The trouble is, not only does the Society lie to outsiders, they regularly lie to their own members! We will consider more of this practice of lying later, but cannot help but quote Revelation 22:15,

"Outside are the dogs and the sorcerers and the immoral persons and the murderers and the idolaters and everyone who loves and practices lying."

While on the Biblical subject of sorcerers, let's also look at Charles Taze Russell and sorcery. Sorcery is defined as *"Divination by the assistance or supposed assistance of evil spirits; magic enchantment; witchcraft."* Sorcerers are usually into astrology as well, looking for patterns and meanings in the stars. Charles Taze Russell was no exception.

In the discourse called *"The Divine Plan of the Ages with Stellar Correspondencies,"* by Grant Jolly, a contemporary of Charles Taze Russell, we find the Society trying to foist the pagan zodiac on its followers. In this discourse, under the heading "The Heavens Declare the Glory of God" we find this statement.:

"...From this we may suppose that the signs (the constellations) of the Zodiac are approximately as old as the human race and perhaps of Divine origin... Indeed the same Bible which points to the Great Pyramid points also to the Heavens as declaring the wonderful plan of salvation... In them (that is, the stars) there is written the hope of

eternal life, which God that cannot lie promised before the world began." (Titus 1:2)

This promise was indeed recorded in the stars before this world began. In considering the Zodiac, it will be necessary to carefully avoid the many errors that have attached themselves in connection with the various heathen religions."

What double talk! The Society takes a completely pagan concept, embraces it, adopts it, goes so far as to compare Jesus Christ to Pisces, even saying,
"...Pisces shall have completely bruised the serpent's head".

The discourse would have done better to have quoted Isaiah 47:13,14 to their eager listeners,

"...Let now the astrologers, Those who prophesy by the stars, Those who predict by the new moons, Stand up and save you from what will come upon you. Behold they have become like stubble, Fire burns them; They cannot deliver themselves from the power of the flame..."

Actually, much of what the early Watchtower Society was involved in could be better called "numerology." Numerology is defined in the dictionary as *"belief in the occult influence of numbers upon the life of an individual."*

The Watchtower taught for many years that the numbers contained in the great pyramid foretold all kinds of events for the human race. They carefully applied every measurement, and translated it into years, months, and days. It is too complex to go into in great detail, so we will consider one example. The Watchtower of June 15, 1922, page 187, supported their "absolute date" of 539 BC by allowing "an inch for a year" in the Great Pyramid of Gizeh. All their other dates are based on this so-called "absolute year" date down until today, and it is false!

This fact sets off a whole string of equally false dates. The year 607 BC for the desolation of Jerusalem and used by Jehovah's Witnesses is therefore likewise false. The "seven times" or "Gentile Times" used by the Jehovah's Witnesses and calculated as 2,520 years is also incorrect and without biblical basis. Their "keystone Year" of 1914, originally set by pyramid calculations, is likewise in error. It will soon be evident to all Jehovah's Witnesses when the generation of 1914 passes on with no fulfillment of their hopes for a new order to be ushered in.

Every Jehovah's Witness should take themselves off to a public library and read up on Pyramidology. They will discover the occult roots of their group and also be surprised to find out how many blatant occult, pagan groups also name 1914 due to pyramid studies.

Modern Jehovah's Witnesses may be surprised to know that Charles Taze Russell wrapped himself in a toga (a pagan Roman garment) prior to his death, and was buried near a pyramid displaying a cross, a crown, and an open Bible! Even in his death he left a memorial of his attempt to fuse paganism with Christianity. Jehovah's Witnesses may visit his grave site for themselves and see.

How sad that the Jehovah's Witnesses are following a false organization, using false dates, and built on false promises. We need to do everything in our power as concerned Christians to make them aware of this deception.

The Consistent Use Of Pagan & Occult Sources Throughout The Watchtower's History

Some Jehovah's Witnesses will try to excuse their founder, Charles Russell, by admitting that he did have some strange doctrines in the beginning, but that the light has grown "brighter and brighter." However, history proves that the Society has consistently used pagan, occult sources to support their doctrines and teachings.

Consider the publication of their *"New World Translation of the Scriptures."* They consistently dishonestly quoted reputable scholars to try to make it appear that they had their support when they did not. The Watchtower Society has the occult view of Jesus Christ, namely that he is "a god," and they altered their "bible" to try and support this distortion of the Scriptures.

Examples are numerous and lengthy and we have covered many of them in our other teaching literature, so will consider only one example here. To support their pagan heresy that Jesus is only "a god," they resorted to quoting a spirit medium for support, with the full knowledge that he was one.

Consider first their distortion of John 1:1 found in their "bible,"

"In (the) beginning the Word was, and the Word was with God, and the Word was *A* god."

For support of this distortion, they turned to the so-called "expertise" of a known spirit-medium. His name was Johannes Greber. He was a defrocked Catholic Priest who received his so-called "translation" of the bible through spiritistic means, usually in trances. The Watchtower Society exposed him in the February 15th, 1956 Watchtower, warning that his sources were demonic. We couldn't agree with them more!

However, in 1961, just five years later, they were singing his praises and quoting him as an authority for their New World Translation, since he was a supporter of their doctrine on the person of Jesus Christ, and all three sources, Greber, the demons, and the Watchtower Society all agreed that Jesus was merely "a god."

While knowingly agreeing with and quoting a spirit medium, they nevertheless spoke out against spiritistic practices. An example is in the October 15th, 1977 Watchtower, on page 624 where they said, *"Since spiritism is condemned by God, it becomes obvious that a person appealing to spiritism for knowledge or help is not appealing to God. He is looking to a source opposed to God..."*

Not a single, reputable Christian or non-Christian scholar would agree with their distortion of John 1:1, in which they called our Savior "a god." The Watchtower has for their support only other Christ-denying cults, the pagans, and the occult for their view of Christ. They do not have the support of the correctly translated Scriptures for their pagan doctrine on Christ. Jehovah's Witnesses need to select a reputable translation of the Bible and read Colossians 2: 8,9;

"See to it that no one takes you captive through philosophy and empty deception, according to the tradition of men, according to the elementary principles of the world, rather than according to Christ. For in Him all the fullness of Deity dwells in bodily form."

All is all, and full is full, and all the fullness of Deity (Godhead, Godship) dwells in Jesus Christ, even in the flesh!

If Jehovah's Witnesses will prayerfully consider this Scripture and begin an examination of a valid Bible by valid scholars, they will come to realize that they have indeed fallen into the trap warned about in this Scripture. They have fallen captive to "empty deception" according to a "tradition of men."

Under the heading of "justified lying" we again turn to the topic of Johannes Greber. After warning against him in 1956, they quoted and followed his teachings from 1961 onwards.

In 1983, only after being cornered with their deception, on page 31 of the April 1st, 1983 Watchtower they denied they knew what they were doing! They promised not to quote him any more, but they left intact his demonic, pagan doctrines on Christ, not only concerning Christ's person, but also the resurrection of our Lord.

Jehovah's Witnesses, do you know that your false doctrine on Christ's resurrection comes directly from demonic sources? Jesus did not have his body dissolved into gases, and then materialize a fake body complete with fake nail-prints to fool His disciples into believing it was really Him risen from the dead!

Let's just take a moment to correct J.W. doctrine from the Scriptures. Luke 24: 36-46 clearly states,

"And while they were telling these things, He Himself stood in their midst. But they were startled and frightened and thought that they were seeing a spirit. And He said to them,

"Why are you troubled, and why do doubts arise in your hearts? See My hands and my feet, that it is I Myself; touch Me and see,

for a spirit does not have flesh and bones as you see that I have." (And when He had said this, He showed them His hands and His feet.)

And while they still could not believe it for joy and were marvelling, He said to them, "Have you anything here to eat?" And they gave Him a piece of a broiled fish; and He took it and ate it in their sight.

Now He said to them, "These are My words which I spoke to you while I was still with you, that all things which are written about Me in the Law of Moses and the Prophets and the Psalms must be fulfilled." Then He opened their minds to understand the Scriptures, and He said to them, "Thus it is written, that the Christ should suffer and rise again from the dead the third day."

Jesus Christ rose bodily, appeared to his followers. It was really Him, and we live because He lives!

Other Doctrines Of Demons

We are warned in 1 Timothy 4:1;

"But the Spirit explicitly says that in later times some will fall away from the faith, paying attention to deceitful spirits and doctrines of demons."

The Jehovah's Witnesses have several other doctrines in common with those received directly from the demons by Johannes Greber, as itemized in his book *"Communication with the Spirit World of God,"* abbreviated to CSW below. We thank the late Bill Cetnar and his wife Joan for their research in this regard, and we are quoting from a list compiled by them in their book *"Questions for Jehovah's Witnesses Who Love the Truth."*

1. Jesus Christ is Not God. *(CSW p.330; J.W. "The Word—Who is He? p. 40).*

2. Jehovah only is God —the Father *(CSW p.302, 331, 328,333: J.W. - "Jehovah" p.8)*

3. Jesus Christ is a created being. *(CSW p.301: J.W. - "Aid to Bible Understanding" p. 918).*

4. Michael is a god. *(Dictionary of Angels: J.W. - " Aid to Bible Understanding" p. 1152).*

5. Christ's body was not resurrected. *(CSW p. 385: J.W. "Things in which It is Impossible For God to Lie" p. 355).*

6. Body of Jesus was dematerialized. *(CSW p. 385: J.W. "Time Is At Hand" p. 129).*

7. There is no Eternal Hell. *(CSW 379: J.W. "Is This Life All There Is?" p. 96).*

8. The Higher Powers of Romans 13 are not earthly governments. *(CSW p. 414, 415: J.W. - "The Watchtower" 1/15/46 p. 27).*

9. The Christian Church is not preaching the Gospel. *(CSW p. 426: J.W. -" Finished Mystery" p. 485).*

Johannes Greber did not like any of the existing translations of the Bible and stated *"...I have used the text as it was given to me by those spirits. "* (The New Testament by Johannes Greber p. 15).

We have to as - Why do Jehovah's Witnesses have so many doctrines in common with the doctrines of these demonic spirits? Why also did Russell expend so much time and energy railing against the demons, while at the same time using their doctrines? Modern Jehovah's Witnesses may not realize that demon manifestations among Watchtower members were quite common during this time. We quote "Zion's Watch Tower" of October 1st, 1907,

"Our understanding is that this great day of the Lord began chronologically in October 1874, and from what we can learn it is since that date that "materializations" have become more and more common... the evidence is too strong to be disputed that there have been numerous genuine manifestations..."

Modern Jehovah's Witnesses may also be surprised to see the date 1874 used in this quote from 1907. It was still used in the 1940's! 1914 is a relatively recent update from 1874, and it itself now needs an update.

Why have the Jehovah's Witnesses deliberately covered over these false dates and also deliberately altered their bible, and then claimed it is accurate, when all evidence is to the contrary? Why also have members overlooked the obvious errors so many times? It can only be that they are under a spirit of deception, and need to have their eyes opened by true light from Jesus Christ. However, they prefer to get their "light" from "angels."

Angels Give Light To The Society
The fact is, Jehovah's Witnesses claim that they receive *"angelic direction"* for their activities.

Their writings from the 1930's are rampant with references to *"angelic direction."* We'll consider a few.

First we must explain that they give their own meaning to the biblical term "remnant" who they consider to be their special "governing body" chosen from those 144,000 members who have a heavenly hope. This "remnant" rules from Brooklyn, New York.

"Vindication," volume III, 1932, page 250 reads,
"...the heavenly messengers or angels of the Lord now used by the Lord in behalf of the remnant. These angels are invisible to human eyes and are there to carry out the orders of the Lord. No doubt they first hear the instruction which the Lord issues to his remnant and then these invisible messengers pass such instruction on to the remnant."

What an admission! The Governing body of Jehovah's Witnesses consisting of several very elderly men, claiming to be "the remnant," form all doctrine for Jehovah's Witnesses. How, you may well ask? According to a book by a former member of the Governing Body, it wasn't by prayer or study of the Bible. *(Crisis of Conscience by Raymond Franz).* It was supposed to be under "angelic direction," but Raymond Franz left because he felt it was a man-made organization.

However, the Watchtower Society has frequently made the claim that all they do is by "angelic direction." By their own admission, this happens invisibly. This is odd, because angels appeared many times to God's chosen ones and were seen.

Since the "remnant" doesn't actually see these angels, by their own admission, what is going on? One can only assume that they "hear voices" or perhaps receive "truths" by "automatic handwriting," or some such procedure.

If this body of men really are the remnant referred to in the Bible, as Jehovah's Witnesses believe, then they must fulfil Revelation 14:5 which speaks of this special group of the 144,000,

"And no lie was found in their mouth; they are blameless."

Not only do we have a history of lying going back over 100 years, but what about these "angels" who direct them?

They do admit they have things "put in their minds". Consider their admission of this in *"Light,"* volume 1, 1930, p. 120.

"Again God put it in the mind of his people, by his angel, to act and to carry out his purposes."

I can't find a single Bible precedent for angels putting things in the minds of believers. The Holy Spirit can motivate us, perhaps at times through our minds, but angels? The warning on angels and men preaching a false gospel has direct application to the Watchtower Society. Galatians 1:8,9 reads,

"But even though we, or an angel from heaven should preach to you a gospel contrary to that which we have preached to you, let him be accursed. As we have said before, so I say again now, if any man is preaching to you a gospel contrary to that which you received, let him be accursed."

What kind of angels are directing the Society and its "gospel"? They are not preaching the same gospel as the apostles, but a contrary one.

Also disturbing is the claim that angels direct the writing of the Watchtower magazine, the prime channel for Jehovah's Witnesses.

"The Lord used the Watchtower to announce these truths. Doubtless he used his invisible deputies to have much to do with it." (Light, Vol. 1, 1930, p. 64).

Did God really send His angels to the Watchtower Organization with these false dates for the end of the world? 1874, 1879, 1914, 1915, 1918, 1925, 1941, 1975? Of course not! If these false dates did not come from God (and they didn't!), can we just then excuse them as "honest mistakes."

No, they cannot be excused on the basis of Jeremiah, chapter 23:16.

"Thus says the LORD of hosts, "Do not listen to the words of the prophets who are prophesying to you. They are leading you into futility. They speak a vision of their own imagination, not from the mouth of the LORD."

Again, the truth of prophecies are shown by their fulfilment, as in Jeremiah 28:9,

"The prophet who prophesies of peace, when the word of the prophet shall come to pass, then that prophet will be known as one whom the LORD has truly sent."

In Biblical times, a prophet whose prophecies failed was taken outside the city gates and "rocked to sleep," or literally, stoned to death.

Jehovah's Witnesses have been misled by false prophets again and again down through their history. This is not of God. Pagan practices, however, always produce false predictions. One has only to read the horoscopes to see how many of the predictions of our modern-day stargazers have failed miserably, proving they never were really inspired.

Jehovah's Witnesses down through the years have adopted pagan practices like numerology, stargazing, the zodiac, false predictions, demonic sources, and deliberate mistranslation of the Scriptures to bolster up their organization's teachings, but their record stands for itself. They are consistently false.

We join with Jeremiah, a true prophet, who chastised the false prophet Hananniah,

"...Listen now, Hannaniah, the LORD has not sent you, and you have made this people trust in a lie."

An Appeal Directly To Jehovah's Witnesses

Sadly, Jehovah's Witnesses have trusted in so many lies, that we do not have the time to detail them all, but we would be pleased to have Jehovah's Witnesses contact us in total confidentiality so they may prove these things for themselves. If they choose, they may dialogue only with those persons who have never been Jehovah's Witnesses, but are concerned enough as Christians to love them dearly, and want to help them come free. We are here to help. We care for you, and we love you enough to tell you the truth.

Do not be ashamed that you have trusted in a lie. The deliberate deceivers are at headquarters. You are not a deliberate deceiver, but one of the deceived. You became a Jehovah's Witness because you truly loved God and wanted to serve Him with your life. It is not too late to turn from this pagan organization masquerading as Christian to real Christianity, found in the person of Jesus Christ.

If you have the right Jesus Christ, you are right for all eternity. If you have the wrong Jesus Christ, you are wrong for all eternity. Any decisions you make now, will count for eternity. Jesus Himself said, **"The thief comes only to steal and kill and destroy; I came that they might have life, and might have it abundantly. I am the good shepherd; the good shepherd lays down His life for the sheep... I am the good shepherd, and I know My own, and My own know Me..."** (John 10:10,11,14).

If you truly love the good shepherd, Jesus Christ, you will not be afraid to come directly to Him, pour out your heart and all your doubts and failings to Him, and allow Him to be the Lord of your life.

Jesus is the door, not the Watchtower Society.
Jesus is the Way, not the Watchtower Society.
Jesus is the Truth, not the Watchtower Society.

Jesus is **"The Way, The Truth, and the Life,"** *(John 14:6).*

If you will lay aside your Watchtower literature in favor of a valid Bible alone, and really seek God with all your heart, you will find Him!

REFERENCES

1. Watchtower, Nov. 15, 1933, p. 334; Nov. 1, 1935, p. 331; Dec. 15, 1987, p. 7

2. Christian Deviations, p. 101

3. Dict. of Cults/Sects, p.149; Kingdom of the Cults, p. 42-43

4. Kingdom of the Cults, p. 39-41

5. The Four Major Cults, by Anthony Hoekema, p. 227

6. Dict. of Cults/Sects, p. 150

7. Watchtower, Mar. 1, 1979, p. 16; July 15, 1960, p. 439; Feb. 15, 1983, p. 12

8. The Golden Age, Joseph Rutherford, p. 252

9. Yearbook of J.W.s 1974, p. 76, p. 145;1975, pps. 245; 1980, pps. 30-31; Cultwatch, p. 81-4; Reasoning from the Scriptures, Rhodes, pps. 339-375; New Light & Governing Body - both whole books.

10. Jehovah's Witness Errors Exposed, by William J. Schell, p. 13

11. Let God Be True, Watchtower B &TS, p. 79

12. Encyclopedia Britannica, 15th edition, pps. 359A, 539, 575; Macropaedia vol. 22, p. 39, 49

13. Crisis of Conscience, Franz, pps. 24-27; Dict. of Cults/Sects, p. 150

14. Kingdom of the Cults, p. 74-5; Aids (WB &TS) pps. 884-5

15. Christian Deviations, p. 107; Dict. of Cults/Sects, p. 154; Kingdom of the Cults, p. 111

16. So What's the Difference, p. 136-7

17. Watchtower, Aug. 15, 1989

18. Depth Exploration in the New Testament, Mantey p. 136-7

19. Governing Body, Watters, p. 61

20. How Not to Translate the Bible, Rowley pps. 41-2

21. Governing Body, Watters, p. 61

22. The Jehovah's Witness New Testament, Countess, pps. 91-3

23. Let God Be True, (WB & TS)

24. Watchout Magazine, March 30, 1975

25. Watchout Magazine, March 30, 1975

26. Governing Body, Watters, pps. 66-7

27. The Bible, the Christian and Jehovah's Witnesses, Lewis, p. 13

28. J.W.'s in the 1st & 20th Centuries, Elliot, p. 16

29. Cultwatch, p. 73, & Apostles of Denial, Gruss, pps. 32-3, 219

30. Combating Mind Control, by Stevens Hassan, p. 56

31. Outline on Winning Witnesses based on a presentation by Carolyn Pemberton, Kingdom Ministries.

32. This is an amended text from a pamphlet by MacGregor Ministries of Canada, used by permission.

RECOMMENDED READING & VIEWING

"Reasoning from the Scriptures with the J. W.s," by Ron Rhodes, (Harvest House)

"The Kingdom of the Cults," by Dr. Walter Martin, (Bethany House)

"Cultwatch," by John Ankerberg & Dr. John Weldon, (Harvest House)

"Christ among other gods," by Erwin W. Lutzer, (Moody)

"Jehovah's Witnesses," by Robert M. Bowman, Jnr, (Zondervan)

"Larson's Book of Cults, "by Bob Larson, (Tyndale)

"Christian Deviations - the Challenge of the Sects," by Horton Davies, (SCM)

"Heresies Exposed," by William C. Irvine, (Pickering & Inglis)

"The Bible, the Christian & Jehovah's Witnesses," by Gordon R. Lewis, (P&R Pub.)

"Thus saith The Governing Body of J. W's," by Randall Watters, (Bethal Ministries)

"New Light," by David Henke, (The Watchman Fellowship)

"Understanding Mind Control Among J. W's," by Randall Watters, (Kingdom Ministries)

Videos; "Witness at your Door," by Jeremiah Films, & "Witness of Jehovah," by Good News Defenders, both available from most Christian video libraries and bookshops.

About the Author:
Selwyn R. Stevens,
Ph.D; D.Min.; M.I.S.D.M.; M.E.A.C.M.

is the President of Jubilee Resources International Inc. a New Zealand-based educational and religious organization involved in informing and equipping Christians of all denominations how to reach the lost and deceived in cults, the occult and secret societies such as Freemasonry. Author of over 35 books (and co-author of two), including twelve Best Sellers, an International Speaker (on five continents) and ordained minister. Dr. Stevens is a third-generation preacher, and has been involved in various Christian groups, and also maintains an active interest in national and world affairs and politics. Dr. Stevens is a Foundation Member of the International Society of Deliverance Ministers, founded by Dr. C. Peter Wagner and convened by Dr. William Sudduth of Virginia, USA; and Apostolic Overseer of the Alliance of African Christian Churches & Ministries based in Zambia. Regular Facebook and e-mail teaching and mentoring is also provided to many Christian leaders across Africa, Asia, Latin America & Caribbean resulting in tens of thousands being equipped for service to the Kingdom of God.

Additional Resources Available by
Selwyn R. Stevens

www.jubileeresources.org (Webshop)
Plus comprehensive range of free tracts to download

Dealing with Curses & Generational Iniquities. This teaching offers hope for all Christians that they can be released into the blessings of God and forever leave behind iniquities and curses that have kept them captive, perhaps their whole families for generations. This explains the twelve major curses that people may have operating in their families, and what to do about them. It also includes new material on the curses over Scottish, English, Irish, Welsh and Scandinavian people, plus many other national and ethnic groups. This teaching has been taught in several nations with much fruit for personal, family and community liberty. Best Seller
Book, E-book, MP4 & DVD

Dealing with Demons: *Insights into evil spiritual influences.* This popular teaching provides outstanding insights regarding evil spiritual influences that exist in the world in which we live today, and then goes further to show us what to do about it. Best Seller
Book, E-book, MP4 & DVD

Insights into Martial Arts, Tai Ch'i TM & Yoga. Much of the western world has seen an explosion of these practices. For many, their involvement has became close to a religion, adopting belief systems, mind sets and practises inconsistent with the teachings of the Bible. Best Seller
Book, E-book, MP4 & DVD

Treated or Tricked - Alternative Health Therapies Diagnosed. Many people are now trying Alternative Health Therapies. This book explains the various medical & spiritual healing methods; investigates whether the "Energy/Life Force" is scientific or spiritual; and describes almost 80 different Alternative Therapies, from Aromatherapy to Zone therapies. Also examines reasons why some are not healed & how to overcome these failures Biblically. Co-authored with Dr. Badu Bediako, (former Assoc. Professor of BioChemistry.) Best Seller
Book, E-book, MP4 & DVD

How to Recognize the Voice of God. How does God communicate to His people? How will you know when it is Him speaking to you? This very practical teaching has already helped many.
Book & DVD

Raising a Blessed Generation. The goals of this teaching are three-fold:
Goal 1: To understand what Blessing is and the Power it has for our lives today;
Goal 2: To Identify and Recover any missed blessings in my own life;
Goal 3: To Begin to Learn How to Bless others, especially our children & grandchildren! Identity and gender confusion is caused by the failure of parents & grandparents to speak identity and destiny into the young ones. Best Seller
Book, E-book, MP4 & DVD

Daniel and the Star Chasers. The counterfeit of Astrology has hidden what God wanted His people to know about the Gospel message in the stars. Daniel taught that truth to the Magi of Asia, and that nearly caused the War of the Continents half a millennium later. Only in recent decades has mankind had the technology to uncover what the Magi saw. Following Daniel's instructions, they went to see the King of Kings and submit their kingdoms and empires to His.
Book, E-book, MP4 & DVD

The Christian Life & the Role of the Fivefold Ministry. The Christian church is being increasingly side-lined in social debate. Have we ceased to be the Salt and Light commanded by Jesus Christ? The Solution: become real Christians! But what does that entail? Then, how are Christians to be governed? God provided the Fivefold ministry to do that. What does that look like? Best Seller
Book, E-book, MP4 & DVD

Help! The Sheep are Escaping: Understanding the Exodus From Church to God's Ecclesia. For most Christians in the West, "church" isn't working! The Old Wineskin cannot compete any longer, as God raises up His New Wineskin to fulfil His end-time purposes. The solution is for "church" to become Ecclesia and for participation with appropriate equipping, releasing and accountability.
Book, E-book, MP4 & DVD

Biblical Healing Training Manual. This thorough examination of Biblical physical healing is the result of many years of experience as well as training under some of the world's best Bible teachers. There are many "How To's", practical prayer and ministry guidelines, reasons why some aren't healed, and what we can do about them, etc. Hundreds have been healed, & many congregations have been empowered to commence regular Healing services with Christ-glorifying results. Best Seller
Book, E-book, MP4 & DVD

Fatal Faith - the Cult Counterfeit of Christianity. This book explains how cults develop and what patterns to avoid. Key Christian and Cult beliefs are compared with the main active cults. How to handle door-knockers, cult exiting, pre-cult spiritually-abusive churches; and how to protect young people from cults. Major ancient & modern heresies examined. Best Seller. *Book, E-book*

The New Age - the Old Lie in a New Package. New Age & Bible beliefs and practices compared, including Reincarnation and Past lives, Astrology, the New Age pseudo Messiah, Self-worship & our Deity-potential. Energy/ Life Forces are examined, and the occult involvement of most holistic health gurus. Best Seller *Book, E-book*

Discerning the Past to See the End Times: *Islam's Role in the Return of Jesus.* The statue in Nebuchadnezzar's dream, interpreted by Daniel, gives us a clear picture of the various empires that have sought domination of the Middle East and beyond. World events circle around this area of vital interest to God and His people. The Bible is a Middle Eastern book, not a European or American book. The context of the empires of the statue give us vital clues about the Empire of the Beast to come! Best Seller *Book, E-book, MP4 & DVD*

Signs & Symbols: Cult, New Age & Occult Insignias & What They Mean. From Ananda Marga, Anarchy, & Ankhs, to Yin & Yang, Yoga & Zodiacs. By popular demand this book has a brief explanation & a Biblical comparison with dozens of insignias. 7th Edition, newly revised. Best Seller *Book, E-book*

How to Minister to Change Lives and Communities. This comprehensive & practical training manual is for those who want to do effective ministry. This can include end-of-service and small-group ministry. Topics include Understanding the Spiritual Realm; Empowerment to Serve; Healing of the Body, & the Soul; Deeper Ministry by appointment & referral; & Biblical blessings to release identity and destiny. Best Seller *Book, E-book, MP4 & DVD*

The Bible 101. A teaching manual introducing the Bible, explaining clearly it's purposes, origins, history, inspiration, symbolism, translations & versions, moving from milk to meat, study helps, rules of interpretation, and how to study it to get the best understanding. *Book, E-book, & MP4*

Insights into Dying, Death & the Destination Options. This teaching has been providing comfort to many people who have been uncertain of their eternal future. This Biblical approach to a frequently misunderstood issue brings hope with joy, or the timely opportunity to make a crucial correction. *Book, E-book, & MP4*

Unmasking Freemasonry - Removing the Hoodwink. Written primarily for the wives & families of Masons to explain the curses brought on themselves and their families through the oaths; then learn how to deal with the effects. History & structure are explained simply. A Past Master who read this book immediately resigned from his Lodge. The prayer guidelines from this book are being used by many ministries worldwide. 7th edition with endorsement by C. Peter Wagner. Best Seller
Book, E-book, MP4 & DVD

Unmasking Mormonism - Who are the Latter-day Saints? Learn about LDS founder Joseph Smith on whose credentials this cult fails Bible tests, the Book of Mormon hoax, Mormon polytheism, true & false priesthood & authority. This book has caused many Mormons to cancel their baptisms & leave to seek the genuine Jesus Christ - the One from the Bible. Best Seller
Book, E-book, MP4 & DVD

Unmasking the Watchtower - Who are the Jehovah's Witnesses? This asks the questions many J.W.'s are being expelled for daring to ask! Check out the changeable prophecies and man-made doctrines of the Watchtower, the authoritarian leaders & their use of Mind-Control & manipulation of members, how to know the One True God, and how you can witness to and pray for a J.W. effectively. Best Seller
Book, E-book, MP4 & DVD

Rome's Anathemas: Insights into the Papal Pantheon. This vital book investigates Constantine's divorce of the Jewish roots of the Christian faith and its replacement with paganism; the Council of Trent rejected the Biblical basis of Luther's Reformation and cursed all who disagreed with them. In John, we read of the marriage feast at Cana. Realizing that the wine was gone and that she herself could not do anything, Mary tells Jesus, because He is the only One who could do something. Mary then gives the stewards her last recorded words and only command - one that we must consider for us to be saved. Mary said, *"Whatever He say to you, do it!"*
Book, E-book, MP4 & DVD

Additional Resources Available by
Selwyn R. Stevens

www.jubileeresources.org (Webshop)
Plus comprehensive range of free tracts to download

Printed in Poland
by Amazon Fulfillment
Poland Sp. z o.o., Wrocław

28350996R00054